The Official Cookbook of
the Chile Pepper Institute

THE OFFICIAL COOKBOOK OF THE

Chile Pepper Institute

PAUL W. BOSLAND & WENDY V. HAMILTON

PHOTOGRAPHS BY CAROLYN GRAHAM

University of New Mexico Press | Albuquerque

Contents

Capsicum chinense

Preface

Come on a chile pepper culinary journey around the world and discover an irresistible collection of recipes! But *The Official Cookbook of the Chile Pepper Institute* is more than just a collection of recipes. It celebrates the rich culinary traditions of chile peppers embraced the whole world over. *The Official Cookbook of the Chile Pepper Institute* is the Chile Pepper Institute's guide to cooking and enjoying chile peppers. It is a celebration of the Institute's Teaching Garden—a unique environment created to present the diversity of chile peppers in a garden setting. The Garden, as it is known by the faculty, students, and visitors to New Mexico State University (NMSU), is an educational facility operating in collaboration with the New Mexico State University's Chile Pepper Breeding and Genetics Program. It is the world's only garden dedicated exclusively to chile peppers and has been an integral part of the Chile Pepper Institute's teaching and outreach programs since 1991.

The Teaching Garden at NMSU is a living classroom where students, scientists, and the public learn about the biology, history, and versatility of the chile pepper. The Teaching Garden makes learning relevant and fun and complements the existing horticulture curriculum at NMSU by providing students with the opportunity to experience concepts taught in the classroom through exploration

(Opposite page)
Garden chile collage.

in the natural world. We have delivered lessons to more than fifty thousand students since the Teaching Garden was first opened to the public. In addition to students, it is visited by gardening groups, scientists from around the world, and our beloved chileheads (fans and devotees of the chile pepper). Most years in excess of fifteen hundred visitors come to the Teaching Garden to learn about chile pepper science, discover the wonders of the many different chile peppers, and hear some of the fascinating stories of their origin and global conquest. Several media outlets have filmed the Teaching Garden, and countless articles have been written about it.

Situated at the historic Fabian Garcia Science Center on the NMSU campus in Las Cruces, New Mexico, the Teaching Garden is easily accessed—one must simply walk through its gate. Once inside, the Teaching Garden provides a beautiful and stimulating outdoor learning experience. Visitors can learn concepts ranging from disease prevention to a chile pepper's heat profile. The space is open every day from June to November; free parking is available next door, in the Fabian Garcia Botanical Garden. At the Teaching Garden's entrance, a mailbox supplies free Teaching Garden maps that assist visitors in identifying the chile peppers. With more than 150 different varieties planted here each year, the map guides one to a specific chile pepper of interest.

For most of the world, the chile pepper is a basic and familiar ingredient, yet there are more than three thousand different varieties across the globe, most of which have not yet been discovered or used by chefs and cooks in the United States. We celebrate the history, culture, and culinary creativity of chile peppers with this useful, appealing, and imaginative book. It will delight those who celebrate the chile pepper culinary culture with fascinating information pertaining to chile peppers and one hundred recipes from around the globe. The distinctive flavors, aromas, and heat profiles of chile peppers are brought to life in a journey around the world experienced as you walk through the Teaching Garden, and as you read this book.

In *The Official Cookbook of the Chile Pepper Institute*, each profiled chile pepper is explored with fascinating information on its origin and use. Peppered throughout are delicious recipes, from baked eggs in stuffed sweet bell peppers to superhot ghost pepper tomato basil soup. This wonderful collection introduces you to the exciting world of chile pepper cooking, covering all the well-known chile pepper varieties and more exotic kinds including the superhots, those chile peppers with one million Scoville Heat Units or more! This book will heat up your cuisine and add flavor to your palate. You will be saying "No Heat-No Love" to your own cooking from now on.

The Chile Pepper Institute is the source par excellence for information on chile peppers, but when you have specific questions about growing them or cooking with them in your locale, contact your local Cooperative Extension Service. Known colloquially as "Extension," the service is a community education agency with offices in most United States counties and territories. Extension offers many free or low-cost educational services that originate from each state or territory's "land-grant university." Information is available in many formats, including publications, videos, online tools, websites, and interaction with master gardeners (volunteers extensively trained to respond to consumer gardening questions). Finding your state's Extension contact information is easy. Go online to: https://nifa.usda.gov/extension and click on your geographic location to access addresses and phone numbers.

Acknowledgments

We dedicate this book to the thousands of visitors to the Chile Pepper Institute who wanted a chile pepper cookbook. Thank you for asking. Writing this book is something we have wanted to do for a very long time. Its publication would never have been possible without the help of many individuals. We would like to thank Fabian Garcia Science Center Superintendent Anthony Aranda for helping keep the Teaching Garden in beautiful condition throughout the season. Research Specialist Ms. Danise Coon for sowing, planting, and overseeing the Teaching Garden. Ms. Amy Goldman Fowler for her thoughtful and generous gift to underwrite the Teaching Garden. A special thanks to Dr. Gary Bachman, Extension/research professor at Coastal Research and Extension Center of Mississippi State University and host and executive producer of the television show *Southern Gardening* for reading and editing the book.

Food photographers can rarely work alone, unless they happen to embody the fortuitous combination of a great cook and skilled camera jockey. Carolyn Graham assembled a small crew to help her work her way through these recipes. Everyone who chipped in did so with a keen sense of adventure for experiencing chiles picante and for supporting this food-filled project in myriad ways. The toque tips begin with Scotty Piper, our temporary in-house culinary student from Kendall College at National Louis University in Chicago, who prepped many of the recipes with great dedication to his craft and whose flair inspired Carolyn to ensure Scotty's skills were captured in every shot. Of course, that is not to diminish the contributions of Carolyn's kiddos and blossoming foodies Kate Graham and Jackson Graham, both of whom pitched in on recipe prep and kitchen cleanup, taste-tested every dish with enthusiasm and a love of spice, held lights and reflectors, and provided hand modeling services when needed. Hugs and bags of New Mexico chiles (as well as a copy of this book) will be delivered to Carolyn's friend Marc Dahlstrom in Spokane, Washington, who generously lent her his photography equipment for this project. And Carolyn's undying love and gratitude goes to her ever-patient spouse, Steve, who joyfully set up lights and tables, steadily held the fork in the shot, made numerous groceries runs, lent a creative eye where needed, and chopped and roasted and fried without complaint or hesitation. Steve's natural skills in the kitchen continue to instill and inspire in Carolyn a deep love of food and drinks and the joy that comes with sharing all of it with family.

Chile peppers are one of the most basic and familiar ingredients known worldwide, yet there are thousands of varieties and probably just as many recipes. This collection represents many of our personal favorites, but we would be amiss if credit were not given to the numerous recipe suggestions from colleagues, students, friends, and family. In the end, it was very difficult to make the final selections. We looked to each recipe as a means to explore the cooking arts of the past, delighting in the present availability of the harvest, and anticipating menu planning in the future. Buen provecho!

Introduction

A stroll through the NMSU Chile Pepper Institute's Teaching Garden in Las Cruces, New Mexico, is both educational and rewarding. At the Teaching Garden, we plan a full year ahead of time because of the wide variety of chile peppers grown and of the necessity to prepare the soil for next year's Teaching Garden. When strolling through the garden, you may see a field of broccoli and marigolds growing next to it. Why the broccoli and marigolds? These plants are useful to control weeds, nematodes, pathogens, and insects using a process called biofumigation. Fresh plant mass is mixed into the soil and releases compounds that suppress soil-borne pests. Biofumigation is important as part of an integrated pest management system, and both broccoli and marigolds have been shown to release effective natural fumigates.

As you stroll through the Teaching Garden, a pattern can be observed. First, the space is laid out by species and then pod types. There are thirty-two known chile pepper species but only five species are domesticated. The terms wild, cultivated, and domesticated are often used with chile peppers, representing a continuum of human-plant relationships.

Wild chile peppers are the plants that were found by ancient peoples when they migrated to the Western Hemisphere. Cultivated chile peppers can be either semidomesticated or domesticated. The

Marigolds and broccoli are planted to control weeds, nematodes, pathogens, and insects in preparation for next season's Teaching Garden.

chiltepin in row 1 at the Teaching Garden is an example of a chile pepper that is both wild and semidomesticated when grown in backyard gardens. In the Teaching Garden, all the named "cultivars" are domesticated chile peppers.

Chile peppers (*Capsicum* species) were one of the first crops in the Western Hemisphere to be domesticated (about 10,000 BCE). They were thought by earlier cultures to possess mystical and spiritual powers, even as they served as food. The person who took the first taste of a chile pepper fruit was rewarded with a burning sensation,

Wild chiltepins in the Teaching Garden.

yet chile peppers began to be worshiped as a gift from the gods. They were held in such high regard by the Aztecs, Mayans, and Incas that these peoples withheld them from their diets when fasting to earn favors and please their gods. The Mayans used chile peppers to treat asthma, coughs, and sore throats. Both Aztecs and Mayans mixed chile peppers with maize flour to produce chillatolli, believed to serve as a remedy for the common cold.

Indigenous peoples in the regions of Mexico, Central America, and South America independently domesticated five of the wild species: the *C. annuum*, *C. baccatum*, *C. chinense*, *C. frutescens*, and *C. pubescens*. The Teaching Garden houses all of them except *C. pubescens*, a species that originated in the highlands of Bolivia and later spread to the Andes where it is often called *locoto* in the Quechua language, or *rocoto* in Spanish. Today it is found from Mexico to Peru in higher cooler elevations. Las Cruces is too hot for it to do well in the Teaching Garden; thus, we do not plant it. Other common names for this species in Spanish are *manzano* and *peron*, because the fruits can be apple- or pear-shaped; it is also sometimes known as *canarios*, because of the fruit's yellow color. In Guatemala, it is called *chamburoto* or *caballo* (horse), because the heat of the fruit kicks like a horse.

Capsicum species are members of the Solanaceae (or Night-shade) family, a large tropical family that includes tomato, potato, tobacco, and petunia. Chile peppers are not related to *Piper nigrum*, the source of black pepper; nor are they related to the Guinea pepper or grains of paradise, *Aframomum melegueta*. One of the puzzling questions about the genus name, *Capsicum*, relates to its origin, which taxonomists have been unable to agree upon. It could stem from the Greek *kapto*, appropriately meaning "to bite," or the Latin *capsa*, meaning "satchel." Some linguists believe that the root is more likely "capsa" because writers before Linnaeus often named plants to indicate a real or a fanciful resemblance to an existing object. Therefore, it is easy to think of chile peppers as a satchel with the chambers inside the pods looking like sacks. Also, *Capsicum* only came to be known to the Europeans after 1492, a time when the classic language of choice would have been Latin, not Greek.

Capsicum annuum varieties are classified by pod types that include bell, jalapeno, serrano, New Mexican, cherry, etc. Despite their vast trait differences, virtually all commercially cultivated *Capsicum* cultivars belong to this species. The ancestor of these species is the wild chiltepin. It has a wide distribution, from South America to southern Arizona, but the cultivated *C. annuum* was first domesticated and grown in Mexico and Central America. By the time the Spanish arrived in Mexico, Aztec plant breeders had already developed dozens of varieties. Undoubtedly, these chile peppers were the precursors to the enormous number of varieties found in Mexico today.

Capsicum baccatum is known in the vernacular as "aji" and has an extended range from southern Brazil west to the Pacific Ocean; it has become a domesticated chile pepper of choice in Bolivia, Ecuador,

Peru, and Chile. In South America, *C. baccatum* is the most grown species. It has cream colored flowers with distinctive yellow, brown, or dark green spots on the flower petals. There are as many different pod types (in relation to shape, color, and size) in *C. baccatum* as in *C. annuum*. Fruits vary in heat from very mild to fiery hot, embodying unique aromatics and flavors. The *C. baccatum* is the chile pepper of choice when making ceviche (marinated fish).

Like all *Capsicum* species, *Capsicum chinense* originated in the Western Hemisphere. However, for some unknown reason, the Dutch physician Nikolaus von Jacquinomist said that he named it after its homeland, China! It is still a mystery as to why he thought China was its place of origin. Because of taxonomic convention that the first name given to a species is used, the misnomer *chinense* is still attached to this Western Hemisphere native species. This is a popular species often grown in Brazil and the Caribbean and other tropical regions. Habanero or Scotch bonnet are well-known pod types of this species. The diversity in fruit shape can equal what is found in the *C. annuum* and *C. baccatum* varieties. The fruit can be extremely hot and aromatic, with persistent heat when eaten. Within this species, the Trinidad Moruga Scorpion has the distinction of being the hottest chile pepper in the world.

Capsicum frutescens has fewer cultivars than *C. baccatum*, *C. chinense*, or *C. annuum*. The reason for this is not clear. The diversity of pod morphology, the difference in pod size, shape, and color results from human selection of which pods to save for the next growing season. It may be that *C. frutescens* grew wild in the same areas as *C. annuum* and *C. chinense*, and humans made the selections from those species instead of *C. frutescens*. One of the best known chile peppers in the world belongs to this species—Tabasco. Indeed, Tabasco hot sauce was named after the hot red fruit that is the central ingredient to this world-recognized condiment. The wild form is known commonly as *melagueta* in Brazil, where it grows wild in the Amazon Basin. The melagueta is not related to the aforementioned *Aframomum melegueta*, the melegueta or Guinea pepper, which is more closely related to ginger. Varieties of *C. frutescens* are grown in Africa, India, and East Asia, where they are called bird peppers. Another favorite is Siling Labuyo, from the Philippines. The leaves of the Sibling Labuyo are used in the Filipino dish *tinola*, made with chicken and papaya.

Chile pepper pod types are a subspecific category that allows for further distinguishing among specific varieties. Pod types such as ancho, bell, jalapeno, pasilla, New Mexican, and yellow wax have specific traits for fresh use, processing, flavor, and heat level. They all belong to the most economically important chile pepper species in the world, *C. annuum*. Many of these *C. annuum* pod types (such as ancho, cayenne, de arbol, guajillo, jalapeno, mirasol, pasilla, poblano, serrano, and yellow wax) are central ingredients in ethnic dishes: ancho and New Mexican for chile rellenos, pasilla for mole sauce, serrano for pico de gallo, and yellow wax for Hungarian goulash.

Pod types can be thought of in the same terms as breeds of dog. It is now commonly accepted that the domestic dog descended from wolves. But among domestic dogs, there are different breeds, such as collie, poodle, chihuahua, etc., each having distinguishing desirable characteristics that make them unique. The same is true with chile peppers: there are species, *C. annuum*, *C. chinense*, etc., and then pod types within the species. Today, several hundred chile pod types (banana, bell, cherry, habanero, aji, ornamental, poblano, cayenne, chiltepin, etc.) are grown worldwide.

Sometimes the name for the pod type is the same as the name of the chile pepper (habanero pod type and habanero pepper). The pod type can be a nickname for several similar varieties (aji pod type and

Aji Lemon, Aji Amarillo, and Aji Mono). And to make things a bit more complicated, a pod name (aji pod type) might describe chile pepper varieties from more than one species (*Capsicum frutescens*—Aji Chuncho and *Capsicum baccatum*—Aji Limon). It can all be a bit confusing. Therefore, we've organized this book's recipes with chile peppers grouped together first by species, then by variety within the species. It will all make perfect sense (and delicious meals) in the end!

Those familiar with chile peppers have noticed the variety of ways in which one sees "chile" spelled. The Chile Pepper Institute has these accepted rules to guide you . . .

- "Chile" with an "e" is the correct spelling of the garden plant and pods, i.e., "the chile pepper."
- "Chili" with an "i" signifies the dish called *chili*, i.e., Texas chili or chili con carne.
- "Chilli" with a double "ll" is the European way of spelling the word meaning the chile pepper dish.

Plurals get even crazier. In the United States the plural is rendered "chilies" (meaning more than one chili dish) and "chiles" (meaning more than one garden chile plant); meanwhile, the British English plural is "chillies."

Recipe Preparation Tips

We love chile peppers in whatever form we can get them, but there is something special about fresh picked peppers: their flavor and texture cannot be duplicated. And, with so many different varieties, they bring bright colors to any summertime meal. So naturally, the first way to handle your garden harvest is to consume as many of the fresh pods as possible. We recommend that you grow or buy a variety of chile peppers, before deciding which ones will become your go-to favorites. Pick fresh, ripe green, red, or rainbow-colored pods, cut them open, smell them, and taste them. We encourage you to taste carefully, by biting a tiny piece from a side wall, avoiding the placenta where the heat (capsaicin) lies.

Chile peppers are very versatile. They can be added raw to everything from dips and salads to pasta dishes or stir-fries. We have provided recipes that call for chile in every format possible—fresh, roasted, frozen, powdered, pickled, and dried. This allows you the flexibility of learning how to handle an over- or -under abundance of pods from your garden or the farmer's market. Also check out our chile infusion section, to learn about varietal heat and flavor before preparing entire recipes. This way you can narrow down or expand your preferences for certain chile peppers and start preparing recipes without the fear of "overheating" your guests.

Some recipes provide guidance on how to prepare chile peppers for specific recipe requirements. An appendix is provided at the back of this book as a quick resource for preparing the most commonly used forms of chile. When you become experienced with the different chile varieties and what they offer a particular dish, you will become comfortable making substitutions of varieties and/or formats (powdered versus fresh; fresh roasted versus canned roasted, etc.), depending on the heat level and flavors desired. As you delve further into your appreciation and preferences for certain varieties, making notes about recipe substitutions, enhancements, and adaptions will prove valuable in future recipe preparations.

The flavors of chile peppers are complex, distinctive, and individualized for each variety. Like the hundreds of flavor profiles in wines, more than two hundred chemical combinations have been identified in chile peppers. These include herbaceous, fruity, vegetal, floral, earthy, sour, lemony, sweet, tropical, smoky, and many, many more.

Knowing and distinguishing among these flavors will set you off on an epicurean adventure. The recipes in this book are designed around the flavor enhancements chile peppers bring to specific dishes.

Chile pepper flavor is created when a specific heat profile combines with its flavor components. One of the most well-known flavor profiles is the "green bell pepper." The chemical producing the characteristic aroma is 2-isobutyl-3-methoxlyprazine, resulting in one of the most potent aromas known to humans. The human nose can detect concentrations of this molecule below the one part per trillion level; in fact, one drop in an Olympic-sized swimming pool full of water will cause the air to smell like a green bell pepper. Each chile pepper has its own unique set of flavor components, giving each pepper its own distinctive flavor. For example, Tabasco has twenty-three flavor components. The habanero has a fruity, apricot-like aroma and flavor that is never forgotten.

In addition, a variety's characteristic "flavor notes" can change (think enhanced or diminished) slightly in a specific variety depending on where and when the chile pepper is grown, much like the terroir associated with wine grapes. These flavor notes are influenced by grilling, roasting, drying, baking, or using the peppers fresh. For example, roasting or grilling a jalapeno will create subtle new volatile flavor components that become recognizable over time and that are not present in the raw pod.

Chile Pepper Heat

Most of us have heard of capsaicin, which is normally the most common component responsible for the chile pepper's heat. However, there are more than twenty-four active related compounds that cause heat in the chile pepper, collectively known as capsaicinoids. These are produced by the glands on the placenta and sometimes on the pod walls. It is these veins in a chile pepper pod that contain the capsaicinoids or heat, not the seeds. Stripping fresh pods of their veins reduces the level of heat experienced when the peppers are added to a recipe. It is only when the seeds encounter the capsaicinoid-filled glands that the seeds may have the heat. Also, when a chef is roasting or grilling chile pepper pods in preparation for freezing, the seeds remaining in the pod will absorb the remaining oil from the veins, thus producing what one might interpret as "seeds with heat."

Any time chile peppers are handled, ALWAYS wear food industry-approved nitrile or latex gloves. Capsaicinoids are incredibly powerful and stable alkaloids, seemingly unaffected by cold or heat while retaining their original potency despite time, cooking, or freezing. Wearing disposable gloves aids in avoiding touching the sensitive parts of your body and receiving an intense burning sensation on your skin or in your eyes.

When preparing recipes using chile peppers, be sure to taste test throughout the process. Tread lightly and err on the side of less is better.

Scoville Heat Units

In 1912 Parke-Davis Pharmaceutical employee Wilbur Scoville had to figure out a way to measure chile pepper heat. The company wanted to standardize their medicinal products that contained the capsaicinoids. Scoville developed a method known today as the Scoville Organoleptic Test. The scale ranges from zero (no heat) all the way into the millions. Scoville heat units (SHUs) are based on a dilution factor, calculated by how much a weighted sample of chile pepper powder must be diluted to the point where one no longer feels the heat at all. Thus, if it takes a 1,000 to 1 dilution, the heat level is 1,000 SHUs; 10,000 to 1 dilution equals 10,000 SHUs. Later, an alternative method was developed using High-Performance Liquid Chromatography (HPLC), which measures heat in parts per million (ppm). Today, that number is multiplied by sixteen to arrive at SHUs. The actual heat of any chile pepper can vary greatly depending on many factors (environment, genetics, location of the fruit on the plant, etc.).

Heat Profile

A lexicon to describe the sensory characteristics of chile pepper heat was developed at the Chile Pepper Institute by one of the authors of this book, Dr. Paul Bosland. Called a "chile pepper heat profile," it includes five descriptive and discriminative attributes: (1) development, (2) duration, (3) location, (4) feeling, and (5) intensity.

Development describes whether the heat builds up immediately or is delayed by five, fifteen, thirty seconds or longer.

Duration is the length of time that one feels the heat sensation. This can be for a brief period, as in disappearing quickly in seconds. Alternatively, the sensation can linger, lasting for many minutes or even hours.

Location refers to where the heat sensation is felt, e.g., the lips; front of the mouth; tip of the tongue; midpalate; or in the throat.

Feeling refers to the sensation of a "sharp" versus a "flat" heat. The sharp heat feels like pins and needles are pricking the tissue, while the flat heat sensation feels like the heat is being coated on with a brush.

Intensity or **heat level** is measured analytically and converted to Scoville Heat Units. In food products, the heat level is labeled as mild, medium, hot, or extra hot, but there are no industry standards for these terms.

Capsicum annuum

Chiltepin/ Chile Piquin

The first chile pepper encountered in the Chile Pepper Institute Teaching Garden is the chiltepin, considered the "mother-of-all-chile-peppers" because it is the original chile pepper. The ancient ancestors of native peoples such as the Aztecs and the Mayans took wild chiltepins and selected for different fruit shapes, colors, flavors, heat levels, and uses, a process that eventually led to the evolution of the numerous pod types we know today.

The chiltepin evolved in and around present-day Bolivia (considered the epicenter of chile peppers) in South America thousands of years ago. The name chiltepin comes from the Aztec language, meaning "flea pepper." Every chile garden needs a chiltepin plant, if for no other reason than it is a great conversation piece.

A close genetically similar variety is named chile piquin. Many people use the names chiltepin and piquin somewhat interchangeably. The word "piquin" possibly originates from the Spanish word *pequeño*, meaning small. The chiltepin is a small round pod varying in length from ¼ to ½ inch. The chile piquin is slightly larger than the chiltepin, is oval shaped, and is considered semidomesticated in central Mexico.

Both pod types mature from green to red, although orange-, yellow-, and brown-colored chiltepins have been found in the wild. The pods are very hot and can be found in stores and farmers' markets in both the pod and powder form.

Both fruits are held erect with a soft pedicel (calyx) trait that allows red ripe fruit to be removed easily from the plant, so frugivorous (fruit eating) birds can easily remove the fruit and eventually disseminate the seeds. The red pod color is attractive to birds, and research has shown that the fruits are spread by birds across the Americas. Indeed, birds developed a symbiotic relationship with chile peppers because their mouths do not have heat receptors to feel the "heat" of a chile pepper. Birds pluck the tiny fruits and pass the seeds through their digestive systems, depositing the seeds wherever they fly, encased in the perfect fertilizer. As a result, chile peppers spread all over South and Central America long before the first peoples settled in the Western Hemisphere. Eventually chile peppers made their way up to the southern United States and all the way down to the southern tip of South America.

Today chiltepins can still be found growing wild in northern Mexico and southern Arizona. In Mexico they have become adapted to growing in the low-range mountain slopes and in some forested areas around Sonora. They grow best at sea level but can thrive in elevations up to twenty-six hundred feet. They prefer shade and live primarily as understory plants in the Mexican and Arizonian Sonoran mountain ranges.

Following the row of chiltepins in the Teaching Garden is a cultivar of chile piquin named NuMex Bailey Piquin, developed at NMSU specifically for mechanical harvesting. A one-row harvester

Freshly harvested NuMex Bailey Piquins.

was also developed at NMSU to shake the plant. An attached conveyor belt then carries the fruits to the rear of the machine for collection. This procedure is like that used to harvest some nut trees.

The NuMex Bailey Piquin was named in honor of the late Mr. Alton L. Bailey, NMSU Extension vegetable specialist, who worked at NMSU from 1958 to 1988 and was a valuable cooperator and actively helped evaluate this selection. The heat of NuMex Bailey Piquin is 97,000 Scoville Heat Units. The heat sensation occurs and dissipates quickly in the mouth. NuMex Bailey Piquin compares favorably with Asian hot chile peppers because it is in the same heat range.

Chiltepins have immediate heat in the midpalate. From there, the heat will move to the tongue, throat, and lips. It builds quickly and then begins to dissipate but lingers on the lips. The flavor of chiltepin is woody, with earthy hints and dried herb tones. In traditional kitchens, chiltepins are pickled when fresh and added to soups and stews. Alternatively, they can be dried or pickled to be used as a year-round spice.

INGREDIENTS

1 cup chiltepins (dried, destemmed, and cooled)

1 tbsp. olive oil

5 garlic cloves (minced)

½ tsp. oregano

½ tsp. freshly ground black pepper

1 tbsp. kosher salt

½ tsp. white vinegar

1 cup boiled water

1 cup cold water

Blue and yellow tortilla chips

Bolivian Chiltepin Salsa

One of the best ways to handle a large quantity of ripe chiltepins or other peppers from your garden is to make fresh salsa. Feel free to experiment with your preferred quantity of peppers. Start with 1 cup and increase or decrease ingredients, as desired.

INSTRUCTIONS

This recipe calls for drying your chiltepins following the harvest. Wash them using a strainer under cold water, destem them, and spread them on a towel to dry or pat them gently. Then, place them on a cookie sheet on the middle rack of an oven preheated at 250°F. Watch them closely for 10 to 20 minutes. The drying time is variable, depending on your oven. When you see the chiltepins just beginning to shrivel, take them out of the oven and let them cool.

Heat the olive oil over medium heat and sauté the peppers for about 30 seconds. Make sure the oil is not hot, because if it is, your salsa will taste bitter. Take the chiltepin peppers and place them in a blender. Add the rest of the ingredients to the blender. Pulse all the ingredients together until you get your preferred consistency. Test the taste of the salsa with a tortilla chip and adjust the salt and black pepper, as needed. Cover and refrigerate for at least 1 hour before serving. Serve in a dipping dish with blue and yellow tortilla chips. Serves 1.

INGREDIENTS

1½ cups water

¼ cup cocoa

1 tbsp. honey

¼ tsp. hot chile powder, such as chiltepin

1 vanilla bean pod for garnish (optional)

Royal (Mayan) Hot Chocolate

It is believed that this delightful and simple-to-make mix was first drunk by the Mayans. It's a nice change from our traditional hot chocolate mix.

INSTRUCTIONS

In a small saucepan, bring the water to a boil. Add the cocoa, honey, and chile powder. Stir to mix. Serve immediately with the vanilla bean as garnish. Serves 1.

Chimayo Landrace/ Heirloom Chile

T he Teaching Garden has, among its other delights, a crop of landrace chile peppers. These include, for example, the Chimayo. Landraces are defined as cultivated, genetically heterogeneous varieties and have evolved in a certain ecogeographical area, where they have adapted to an area's climatic environment, growing conditions, and traditional uses. Landraces, which at first seem to be frozen in time, are in fact in a constant state of evolution because of natural and artificial selection. Many landraces have disappeared from cultivation but there are a handful of northern New Mexico landraces that have been continuously grown for several hundred years in the same locales. Their unique strength is that they have adapted to shorter growing seasons than the chile varieties grown in southern New Mexico. Four of northern New Mexico's more famous landraces, Chimayo, Dixon, Espanola, and Valerde, have been grown within the villages that bear their names. Today, farmers produce these chile peppers on small plots of land. Landrace populations are often variable in appearance, but they can be identified by their overall appearance and have a certain genetic similarity. Typically, northern New Mexico landrace chile peppers are about 6 inches long or shorter with crinkly skin. The chile pepper is eaten fresh, either red or green, or

(Opposite page) Chimayo green and red chile fruits on a plant in the Teaching Garden.

dried whole and ground into a coarse powder. Because of the small volume of production, the great majority of the New Mexican landrace chile peppers and powders are consumed locally.

Some landraces were hybridized together to create the New Mexican pod type. Espanola Improved is one such variety. Although yields may not be as high as for other chile peppers, the stability of landraces in the face of adverse conditions is typically high. As a result, new pests or diseases may affect some but not all the individuals in the population. A medium hot chile with 5- to 6-inch pods, Espanola Improved was developed in 1983 by Frank Matta and Roy Nakayama at the NMSU Alcalde Agricultural Science Center, near Espanola, New Mexico. Espanola Improved is like Chimayo in that it matures early and has the same fruit characteristics. However, it is more uniform and better yielding than Chimayo. In 2021 this variety was grown by astronauts aboard the International Space Station. NASA astronaut K. Megan McArthur described these chile peppers as having "a nice spiciness and a bit of a lingering burn."

While landrace varieties can literally be one thousand years old, another type of chile pepper is the heirloom chile pepper, which is an old cultivar, released to the public at least fifty years ago and maintained by gardeners and farmers. It differs from a landrace in that an heirloom could have been bred in another locale and brought to a community. Over time, heirlooms can become landraces, but normally the seeds are saved from plants that are true-to-type. There can be less variability in heirloom pods as compared to a landrace. Heirloom cultivars in the Teaching Garden include Bulgarian Carrot, Barker's Hot, Pimento L, and Floral Gem.

Calabacitas

Calabacitas is a traditional New Mexico fall recipe using seasonal garden ingredients, including landrace or heirloom green chile, corn, and squash. For variation, toss in some fresh, chopped tomatoes or top the dish with cheddar cheese. For a one-pot meal, cook up some ground beef or chicken and add the vegetables to the meat or poultry.

INSTRUCTIONS

In a large skillet, heat the oil over medium low heat. Add the onion and sauté for 2 minutes. Add the squash and sauté for 5 minutes or until the squash just starts to soften.

Flip the squash over occasionally to ensure that all of it cooks. Add the corn, green chile, oregano, salt, and pepper. Cook for 2 minutes. Taste and add more salt, if needed. Let rest a minute or two before serving. Serves 4 to 6.

INGREDIENTS

1 tbsp. canola oil *or* olive oil

½ cup onion (minced)

1 lb. yellow squash or zucchini, other summer squash, *or* a combination of two or more (cut into ¼-inch slices)

1 cup corn (fresh, frozen, or canned)

½ cup Chimayo, Dixon, Velarde, *or* other fresh green chile (roasted, peeled, deveined, deseeded, and chopped)

1 tsp. fresh Mexican oregano *or* ½ tsp. dried oregano.

Salt to taste

A couple shakes of pepper

INGREDIENTS

3 tbsps. vegetable oil

2 cups yellow onions (finely chopped)

1 garlic clove (finely chopped)

1 tbsp. flour

2 to 3 cups chicken broth

1 cup green NuMex Heritage Big Jim *or* NuMex Big Jim chiles (roasted, peeled, deveined, deseeded, and chopped)

New Mexico Green Chile Sauce

Green chile sauce is a classic, all-purpose sauce basic to New Mexican cuisine. It's at its best when made with fresh roasted New Mexican–grown green chiles, but frozen green chile can be used as well. Traditionally, this sauce is used over enchiladas, burritos, and chile rellenos.

INSTRUCTIONS

Heat a skillet over medium heat. Add the oil and when hot, add the onion and garlic. Sauté until soft. Stir in the flour and blend well. Simmer for a couple of minutes to cook the flour, being careful not to brown it. Slowly add the broth and stir until smooth. Add the remaining ingredients. Bring to a boil and reduce the heat. Simmer until the sauce has thickened, about 15 minutes. Taste and adjust the seasonings. The sauce will keep for about 5 days in the refrigerator and freezes well. The heat level depends on the variety of chile peppers used and the amount added. Makes 2 to 3 cups.

Ornamental Chile

The question most asked about ornamental chile peppers is "are they edible?" The answer is "yes." There are no toxic chile peppers. However, the flavors and aromas developed in other chile pepper pod types are normally missing in ornamental chile peppers. Still, most have heat, so they can spice up a dish of soup.

Ornamental chile peppers are also an innovative way for small and hobby farmers to produce a high-value alternative crop. In recent years, ornamental chile pepper plants have been sold in local grocery stores, nurseries, or florist centers for suggested use as a colorful bedding, houseplant, table centerpiece, or holiday celebratory plant. They can be planted outdoors as long as weather permits. Ornamental chile peppers are drought and heat tolerant, making them perfect for the looming climate change.

Historically, chile peppers were highly regarded as ornamental plants. From the fifteenth century in Europe to the twentieth century in the United States, they were valued as a Christmas gift plant because of the association of their green and red fruits with the holiday. In the 1950s poinsettia breeding changed the phenotype of the poinsettia from a cut flower to a potted plant, making it a more popular decorative plant during the Christmas season, and peppers were relegated to a minor crop in the greenhouse potted plant industry.

(Opposite page) NuMex Easter ornamental peppers, 2014 All American Selection winner.

In the Teaching Garden, there are three types of ornamental chile pepper plants: (1) garden or border, (2) potted, and (3) florist type. NuMex Centennial and NuMex Twilight are two examples of chile peppers used in a formal garden or a flower bed in the landscape.

These selections are taller than those used in the potted nursery industry and are mostly used as landscape garden accents, borders, and hedge plants. NuMex Centennial and NuMex Twilight are piquin-type chile peppers with multicolor fruit. The fruit begins as purple and ripens through to yellow, orange, and then red. NuMex Twilight has white flowers and green leaves, while NuMex Centennial has purple flowers and purplish foliage. The yellow fruit stage is more pronounced in NuMex Twilight.

The potted ornamental chile pepper is usually a compact plant with showy fruit that grows well in containers. Unlike standard chile pepper cultivars that have a dichotomous growth pattern, ornamentals have multiple stems branching from the basal stems, giving each plant a shorter, more compact growth habit ideal for potted plants.

The NMSU chile pepper breeding program has been developing dwarf ornamental cultivars since 1995. The NMSU "Holiday" series of ornamental cultivars reflects holidays represented by the colors of the fruits. For example, NuMex St. Patrick's Day has green to orange fruit with white flowers, the colors of the flag of Ireland. Currently, sixteen NMSU Holiday cultivars are available, in all the colors of the rainbow.

The last type of ornamental chile pepper displayed in the Teaching Garden is the florist type. This cut stem type is a popular chile pepper in Europe and has only recently become popular in the United States. NuMex Mirasol was bred to be used as a cut stem. The cut stems of these ornamental chile peppers add color and texture to mixed bouquets. The florist types have a tall stem with well-displayed fruits.

NuMex Twilight.

NuMex Mirasol has a very nice presentation of red fruit clusters. With this class of ornamental chile peppers, the fruit is upright, and the leaves can be easily removed from the stems.

These uniquely beautiful chile peppers can be very hot. For example, NuMex Twilight can measure in at 30,000 to 50,000 SHUs, equaling a cayenne. Just in case you want to experiment with ornamentals in your dishes, we have provided you with a couple of different recipes using these cultivars.

Tortilla Soup with a Color Twist

There are so many ways to make this hearty "dry"— referring to the dry tortilla ingredient that absorbs some of the stock—soup. Add a few of your fresh-picked garden ornamental peppers for a splash of color.

INGREDIENTS

2 tomatoes (halved)

2 tbsps. olive oil

1 medium onion (chopped)

2 garlic cloves (chopped)

4 cups chicken stock

Oil for deep–frying

12 corn tortillas (preferably a little stale)

2 to 3 pasilla chiles (deveined, deseeded, and chopped)

Salt and pepper to taste

Small handful of ornamental chiles, avocado slices, and sour cream for garnish

INSTRUCTIONS

Preheat your oven broiler. Arrange the tomato slices, cut sides up, in a broiler pan. Broil tomatoes 5 to 7 minutes, until they begin to brown. Remove from broiler and set aside. Heat half of the olive oil in a frying pan. Add the onion and garlic and sauté for 5 to 7 minutes until softened and golden brown. Carefully tip the contents of the pan into a blender or food processor, add the broiled tomatoes, and process to a puree. Heat the remaining olive oil in the pan and cook the pureed tomato mixture until thick, stirring constantly. Stir in the chicken stock and bring to a boil, then reduce the heat and simmer for 30 minutes. While the soup is simmering, heat the oil for deep frying. Cut the tortillas into 2½-inch strips. Add the chopped pasilla chiles into the oil and deep fry with the tortilla strips until the strips are crisp and brown and the chiles are crumbly (about 3 to 5 minutes). Lift ingredients out and drain on a paper towel. Season the soup with salt and pepper. Ladle the crisp tortillas and chiles into warm bowls. Ladle the soup on top. Garnish with a few colorful ornamental chiles, avocado slices, and sour cream. Serve immediately. Serves 4.

Ornamental Chiles in Floral Arrangements

In addition to giving your favorite dish a splash of color, ornamental chile peppers can brighten your dinner table. Experiment with cutting a few branches of your favorite ornamental pepper branches and presenting them in your favorite vase. Be sure to make your cuttings just as the pods reach their full color change and follow the instructions below to extend their freshness as long as possible in your indoor arrangement.

INSTRUCTIONS

Plan to cut your ornamental chile stems as early as possible in the morning when temperatures are still cool and plants do not feel the stress from warming daytime temperatures. Using a sharp pair of floral shears, cut the stems on plants whose pods have just matured to their full color and whose leaves are unaffected by disease. Cut the stems at a 45° angle. Because these stems are naturally short, you may not have enough discretionary length to cut them again at a slightly shorter length before placing them in your vase, so it's important to cut them the first time at 45°: cutting on an angle increases the surface area for water intake. Place each cutting in your collection basket so as not to harm the stems, pods, or leaves

Ornamental pepper stems from your garden (your arrangement will determine the number needed)

Other garden floral stems (optional)

Clean and appropriately sized vase

Fresh clean room temperature water

Sharp floral shears

Collection basket for carrying stems back into your home

Sink with drain plug

1 to 2 drops Dawn liquid soap

Vase marbles *or* 1–inch smooth rocks (enough to fill bottom of floral vase)

1 cup 7–UP (this makes the water slightly acidic, letting the water travel up the stems more rapidly than basic water. The sugar is a food source, keeping the flowers hydrated and fresh.)

1 to 2 drops liquid bleach

while collecting the rest of your floral arrangement stems.

Immediately upon completing your stem gathering, return indoors and fill your sink with enough fresh clean room temperature water and a couple drops of Dawn liquid soap to cover your stems completely. The liquid soap will ensure that any insects coming inside on your stems are removed. Stir the water a couple times with your hands to be sure the soap is mixed with the water. Then gently place all your stems in the sink, carefully making sure all floral content is completely submerged. While soaking the stems, add the marbles or smooth rocks to your vase. Mix the 7-UP and a couple of drops of bleach in a cup or bowl to fight bacterial growth. Pour this mixture into the vase. Add water to fill the vase at least halfway. Gently rinse your stems under the faucet or fill a second sink with clean, room-temperature water to rinse your stems. Add your floral stems to the vase and arrange to your satisfaction. Fill the remainder of the vase with water.

Bell

Bell peppers, or bells, as they are commonly called, are probably the best-known group of chile peppers and may be the most economically important pepper grown in the United States. California, Florida, and Georgia are the three largest producers of bell peppers in the United States; however, more than 70 percent of the world's bell peppers are produced in Asia. Bell peppers also have the largest number of cultivars of any *Capsicum* genus, with more than two hundred cultivars bred. In the Teaching Garden, the bells are selected based on color, heat, disease resistance, and availability to the home grower.

The term *bell peppers* refers to fruits that are blocky, with a square shape and a flat bottom. California Wonder is one of the oldest cultivars and is typical of the pod type. In Europe, one finds an elongated bell pepper, La Muyo. The most distinguishing characteristics of La Muyo are the non-flat bottom and two-to-three celled fruits, instead of the four-celled pod found in the North American types. In early America, the bell pepper was known as the bullnose pepper and was grown by Thomas Jefferson. In 1812 Jefferson recorded bullnose peppers on his garden calendar at Monticello. They were called bullnose peppers because of the illusion of the tip of the pod resembling a bull's nose. Bell pepper cultivars can begin as green, purple, yellow, or white and ripen to shades of red, orange, yellow, green, and brown. They generally have no heat but have some wonderful flavors. The most familiar is a green bell's flavor. Purple bells have a tannic note, while red, yellow, and orange bells are slightly sweeter than green bells. There is also a cultivar that is mildly hot, namely, Mexibell.

Bell peppers are very high in vitamin C, and one bell pepper may provide up to 169 percent of the Recommended Daily Allowance (RDA) of this vitamin. Other vitamins and minerals found in bell peppers include vitamin K1, vitamin E, vitamin A, folate, and potassium. One study took a close look at vitamin C, vitamin E, and six carotenoids (alpha-carotene, beta-carotene, lycopene, lutein, cryptoxanthin and zeaxanthin) and found that bell peppers contained at least two-thirds of all the listed nutrients. Bell peppers alone provided 12 percent of the total zeaxanthin found in the study participants' diets. They also provided 7 percent of the daily vitamin C recommendations. Recent studies have shown that both the vitamin C content and the carotenoid content of bell peppers increase with ripening. When the vitamin C and carotenoid content of bell peppers increases, so does their total antioxidant capacity, which can be a source of great health benefits. A good rule of thumb is to judge bell peppers less by their basic color and more by their color quality, overall texture, and feel. Whether green, red, yellow, or orange, optimally ripe bell peppers will feel heavy for their size and be firm enough to yield only slightly to pressure.

Bell peppers can also be valuable sources of health-supportive sulfur compounds. Several recent studies have taken a close look at the presence of enzymes called cysteine S-conjugate beta-lyases. These enzymes play a vital role in the sulfur-containing metabolic pathway, the thiomethyl shunt. Laboratory studies have shown these enzymes reduce cancer risk.

Baked Eggs in Stuffed Sweet Bell Peppers

Make your Sunday morning brunch extra special with this delightful twist on eggs.

INSTRUCTIONS

Preheat the oven to 400°F. Cut the peppers in half and remove ribs and seeds. Place cut side up in a shallow microwave safe bowl or dish. Add ⅓ cup water to bowl. Sprinkle the peppers with kosher salt and cover with a microwave-suitable lid. Microwave on high for 5 minutes. Remove and set aside. Heat a large skillet over medium high heat and melt the butter and olive oil. Add the garlic and cook for 1 minute, stirring after 30 seconds. Add the onion and sauté for 2 to 3 minutes, stirring occasionally. Add the butternut squash, thyme leaves, and kosher salt and cook for another 5 minutes. Remove from the heat. Add the brandy. Return to the heat and cook for 4 to 5 more minutes until the brandy has cooked down and the squash has softened and is easily pierced with a fork. Keep warm and add the ricotta and Feta cheese. Taste and season with more salt, if desired. Pour the marinara sauce in the bottom of a 9-inch x 12-inch baking dish. Place the peppers cut side up and spoon ½ to ¾ cup of butternut squash mixture

INGREDIENTS

3 large bell peppers

⅓ cup water

Kosher salt

2 tbsps. butter

1 tbsp. olive oil

2 garlic cloves (diced)

½ cup onion (chopped)

1 lb. butternut squash (peeled, deseeded, and cut into ½–inch pieces)

1 tsp. dried thyme leaves

¼ cup brandy

½ cup ricotta cheese

¼ cup crumbled Feta cheese

2 cups marinara sauce

6 eggs

Freshly ground black pepper

into each pepper, creating a hollow for the eggs. Bake the peppers and squash mixture for ten minutes or until warmed through. Remove from oven. Carefully break the eggs into a small ramekin or measuring cup and slowly pour into each pepper, taking care not to overflow the egg. Repeat until each pepper is filled. Season with freshly ground black pepper and bake the peppers for 10 to 12 minutes or until the egg whites are set. Serve each pepper with marinara sauce and extra Feta cheese, if desired. Serves 6.

INGREDIENTS

¾ cup extra-virgin olive oil, divided

6 garlic cloves (thinly sliced)

6 medium yellow onions (sliced ¼-inch thick)

6 large bell peppers (deveined, deseeded, and sliced lengthwise ½-inch thick)

1 cup pureed tomatoes

1 sprig basil *or* oregano

Kosher salt

1 tbsp. white wine vinegar *or* red wine vinegar

Peperonata

This delicious summer side dish features a bountiful quantity of bell peppers, making it a great recipe to use when your peppers all ripen at the same time. Serve with roasted meats or over a bed of rice. It is recommended that you cook this dish slowly, as the low heat tends to enhance the flavors.

INSTRUCTIONS

In a large pot or Dutch oven, heat ½ cup olive oil over medium heat until shimmering. Add the garlic and cook, stirring, until just starting to turn golden, 3 to 4 minutes. Stir in the onions, increase the heat to medium-high, and cook for 2 minutes. Stir in the peppers and cook, stirring occasionally, until starting to soften, about 20 minutes. Add the tomatoes and basil or oregano sprigs and stir to combine. Bring to a gentle simmer, then lower the heat to maintain a simmer. Continue to cook, stirring occasionally, until the peppers are very soft, about 1 hour. Stir in remaining ¼ cup olive oil and season with salt. Stir in the vinegar. Discard the herb sprigs. Serve right away, or chill and then serve reheated, slightly chilled, or at room temperature. Serves 4 to 8.

Pimiento/ Pimento

Next in our walk through the Teaching Garden is the pimiento, sometimes spelled pimento. This is our second no-heat pepper, which can be grown instead of bell peppers or in addition to them if you prefer an even sweeter flavor. Initially imported from Spain, they were first grown in Spalding County, Georgia, in 1911. Mr. S. D. Riegel developed a line of pimientos named Perfection Pimiento and released it in his 1914 *Riegel Seed Catalog*. The catalog cited Perfection Pimiento as the sport (mutation) of a cultivar received from Valencia, Spain.

There are generally two types of pimientos grown in the United States: the oblate fruit or tomato type and the conical or heart-shaped fruit. Tomato type cultivars are Sunnybrook and Early Sweet Pimiento, while Perfection and Pimiento L are cultivars of the conical shaped fruit type. Both Perfection and Pimiento L are two of the best-known heirloom cultivars; both produce lots of fruit under high-temperature conditions. Pimientos taste great fresh in salads and as an ingredient in pimiento cheese; they are also wonderful for stuffing olives.

New Mexican-Style Potato Salad

When this recipe floated to the top of the recipe pile, it was destined to become the perfect salad for the next park picnic.

INSTRUCTIONS

Boil the potatoes until fork tender, remove from water, and let cool until they can be held to peel. Cut the potatoes into bite size chunks. In a large bowl, combine the potatoes, eggs, onion, pimientos, and chile pepper. Combine the mayonnaise, lime juice, salsa, and seasonings. Add to the potato salad and mix until well blended. If desired, add more mayonnaise and garnish with cilantro or parsley. Note: Warm potatoes gain and hold flavors better than if you let them cool completely prior to mixing with other ingredients. Serves 8 to 10.

INGREDIENTS

5 lbs. potatoes

4 hardboiled eggs (chopped)

1 medium sweet onion (finely chopped)

One 2-oz. jar diced pimientos

1 large green Espanola Improved *or* NuMex Sandia Select chile (roasted, peeled, deveined, deseeded, and chopped) *or* one 40-oz. can chopped green chile

1 cup mayonnaise

1 tbsp. fresh lime juice

½ cup salsa

1 tsp. salt

½ tsp. ground black pepper

Fresh cilantro *or* parsley (chopped, optional)

¼ cup achiote seeds

2 cups extra virgin olive oil

YELLOW RICE

2 tbsp. achiote oil

½ cup yellow onion, chopped

½ cup finely chopped green pepper

1 bay leaf

½ tsp. salt

1 tsp. ground pepper

2 cloves garlic, minced

½ cup canned petite–diced tomatoes, no salt added (drain well)

1 cup long–grain white rice, rinsed well and drained

1⅔ cups low sodium chicken broth

⅔ cup frozen peas

⅓ cup chopped drained pimentos (one 4–oz. jar)

2 tbsp. parsley for garnish

Latin American Yellow Rice with Achiote Oil

This Latin American recipe is a festive side dish, full of color and flavor. You may be familiar with rice recipes that add saffron to rice to create a yellow color. Here we are using achiote (or Annatto) seed oil. This is an infused olive oil that absorbs the flavor of the seeds. Achiote oil is easy to make (see instructions below) and can be stored in the refrigerator for up to 2 weeks.

INSTRUCTIONS FOR OIL

Add the achiote seeds and olive oil to a small skillet. Cook over medium heat until the oil is warm. Reduce the heat to low and let the seeds infuse the oil for 2 to 5 minutes. Remove from the heat and let cool for 30 minutes. Strain the oil and toss any remaining seeds.

INSTRUCTIONS FOR RICE DISH

In a medium saucepan, heat the achiote oil until simmering. Add the onion, green pepper, bay leaf, salt, and pepper. Cook, stirring frequently, until the vegetables begin to soften, about 3 minutes. Add the garlic and cook until fragrant, about 40 seconds. Add the tomatoes and cook, stirring occasionally, until the vegetables are very soft and fragrant, about

2 minutes. Add the rice and cook, stirring constantly to prevent sticking to the pan, until well-coated with the vegetables and achiote oil, about 1 minute. Add the broth and stir. Bring to a boil. Reduce the heat to very low, cover, and let simmer for 15 minutes. Add the peas and replace the cover. Remove from the heat and let rest until the liquid has been absorbed and the rice is tender, about 15 minutes. Remove the bay leaf. Add the pimentos and fluff the rice with a fork. Garnish with parsley, if desired. Serve warm. Serves 6.

New Mexican

T he New Mexican pod types are where the fun begins in the Teaching Garden. The history and heritage of these chile peppers led to the creation of the uniform "New Mexican" pod, and fueled the "Mexican" food industry in the United States. Until the mid-twentieth century, chile peppers were a regional kitchen garden plant—homegrown and home-cooked.

Historic documentation notes that Mexican chile peppers were introduced to the Pueblo Indians of New Mexico in 1540 by Francisco Vasquez de Coronado. The Spanish conquistador introduced both the pepper seeds and the Spanish way of farming. The Pueblo Indians irrigated their chile peppers with water from the Rio Chama. To this day, family farms plant specific varieties of chile seeds passed down through families and neighbors.

The creation of the New Mexican pod type ignited an explosion of food uses in what was, and is still today, called "Mexican" by the United States food industry. Interestingly though, the people of the state of New Mexico call their cuisine "New Mexican." In 1913, following nine years of development, Dr. Fabian Garcia, director of the NMSU Agricultural Experiment Station in Las Cruces, released the first NMSU chile cultivar. It was named New Mexico No. 9; with its development, the world was introduced to a new chile pepper pod type. The New Mexican pod type is the basis for green chile, red chile, and much of the paprika production in the world today. Dr. Garcia's original New Mexican pods have been continuously bred for refined qualities of varying heat levels, flavor attributes, sizes, and skin thicknesses since 1913.

Beginning in 1975 and continuing today, the trademarked moniker "NuMex" is the "first" name on any chile pepper cultivar developed at NMSU. The first cultivar to carry the NuMex moniker was NuMex Big Jim. Currently, there are more than fifty different chile pepper cultivars that do so.

When the New Mexican pod type was first introduced, it became the "go-to" chile pepper that could do it all. It became commonly used in salsa, hot sauce, enchilada sauce (green or red), stuffed peppers, and so on. No longer were specific chile peppers required for specific dishes or sauces. One pod type did it all. The creation and development of the New Mexican pod type changed the food landscape of the United States forever. It explains the increasing popularity of the green to red New Mexican chile pepper sold across the United States in the fall of each year. Although all New Mexican pod types share a similar pod shape and size, they differ a great deal in color, flavor, heat, nutritional properties, and uses.

The New Mexican–type chile is also called "long green" or "Anaheim." The Anaheim seed originated from New Mexico No. 9 grown in New Mexico and was brought to California in 1896. Therefore, the Anaheim cultivar is a New Mexican pod type. Today, in the produce industry, "Anaheim" means mild, while "New Mexican" means a hotter pod.

Hatch chile peppers are an enigma in the chile pepper industry. This is a name associated with the town of Hatch in southern New Mexico. Many are under the impression that when buying Hatch green chile peppers, they are buying chile peppers from this town.

NewMex Heritage
Big Jim fruits.

However, there is no cultivar named "Hatch." In fact, any chile pepper can legally be sold as Hatch even if grown in another state or country. To complicate the matter, there is a Hatch brand of canned chile peppers processed in Deming, New Mexico, which owns the trademark name "Hatch." This brand has been on the market for years, but most of these chile peppers are grown in Mexico, not Hatch, New Mexico. The chile pepper crop area in Hatch is insufficient to supply all the sellers claiming to provide "Hatch chile."

Green Chile Rellenos

Quintessential to the unique New Mexican cuisine, green chile rellenos are a staple of what it means to enjoy southwestern gastronomy.

INSTRUCTIONS

Heat the butter in a skillet over medium heat and sauté the onion and garlic until soft. Add the oregano and cook for an additional 5 minutes. Remove from the heat and stir in the sour cream and cheese. Make a slit in the side of each chile and stuff with the cheese and sour cream mixture. Dredge the chiles in flour and shake off any excess. Beat the egg whites until they form stiff peaks. Beat the yolks with the water, 3 tbsp. of flour, and salt. Fold the yolks into the whites and stir gently. Dip the chiles in the egg batter and fry one at a time in 1 to 2 inches of oil until they are golden brown. Serve covered with your favorite New Mexican sauce. Serves 6.

INGREDIENTS

2 tbsps. butter

1 medium onion (chopped)

2 garlic cloves (minced)

1 tsp. dried oregano

½ cup sour cream

6 oz. cheddar cheese (cubed)

6 New Mexican green chiles (roasted and peeled)

Flour for dredging

3 eggs (separated)

1 tbsp. water

3 tbsps. flour

¼ tsp. salt

Vegetable oil for frying

New Mexican green chile sauce

Green Chile Cheeseburger

This is a favorite comfort food at restaurants any time of year but especially in the late summer, when the local chile harvest fills the air with the scent of roasting chiles. Many New Mexicans can never get enough green chile cheeseburgers.

INSTRUCTIONS

In a mixing bowl, combine the ground beef, salt, cumin, and chile powder. Mix by hand to combine. Then form into four hamburger patties. Set aside. Preheat your grill to 350°F, place the whole chile pods on the grill, turning occasionally until both sides are blackened (about 5 minutes each side). Remove the chile pods from the grill and place them in a tightly sealed glass container or enclose them in a brown paper bag. The steam will loosen the chile skins in about 10 minutes. Place under tap water to easily remove the skins. Slice the chiles open lengthwise and remove the veins and seeds. Set aside. Place the hamburgers on the grill and cook each side for about 5 minutes or until desired doneness. One minute before removing the patties from the grill, place 2 strips of chile and 1 slice of cheese (in that order) on top of each burger. Allow the cheese to melt over the chiles. Place each patty on a hamburger bun, top with your favorite toppings, and enjoy! Serves 4.

INGREDIENTS

1½ lbs. ground beef

1 tsp. salt

1 tsp. cumin

1 tsp. chile powder

4 New Mexican fresh green chiles

1 medium yellow onion (sliced into thin slices)

4 slices cheese (pick your favorite)

4 hamburger buns

Toppings

Paprika

"Paprika'" is a term that can be confusing, so we will take an extra moment to point out three very different pepper varieties used to make "paprika."

In the United States and in global trade, "paprika" refers to a no-heat bright red powder or flaky spice used mainly as a decorative topping on many dishes, including creamed onions, baked potatoes, and deviled eggs. Paprika is made from any variety of *C. annuum* that has little-to-no heat and retains a bright red color. This same no-heat, red powder is also used as a coloring agent (think red lipstick).

In Hungary, the word "paprika" is used to describe a variety of sweet, smoked, and/or hot *Capsicum* peppers that add flavor and heat to many Hungarian dishes. Paprika can be chopped, stuffed, or ground into a fine powder and can be quite hot. It has been referred to as "red gold" by Hungarian farmers. Hungarian paprika is treasured for its unique flavors, pod dimensions, and heat levels.

Furthermore, in Hungary, paprika can be either round or long, conical, and pointed; some are shaped like tomatoes. Traditionally, to make Hungarian paprika, fruits are strung together and hung to air dry. After the fruits are dry, they are destemmed, deseeded, and ground.

Finally, Spanish or Moroccan paprika is dark red and has the

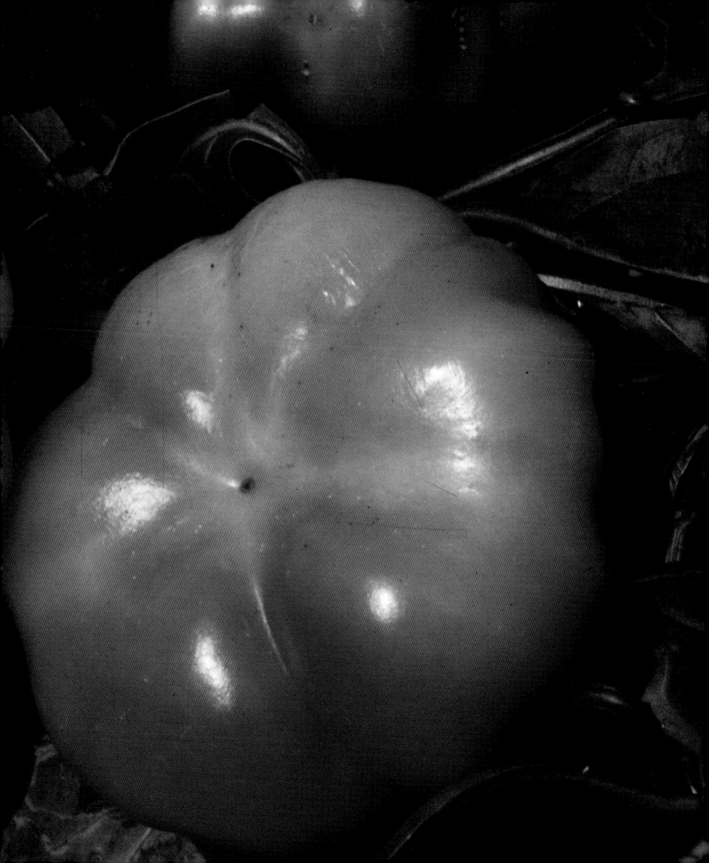

shape and size of a small ball; thus, it is commonly known as "bola." The basic types in Spain are "dulce" (sweet, no heat), "ocal" or "agirdulce" (bittersweet with a slight heat), and picante (hot, with a noticeable heat level). The three qualities of Spanish paprika are the "extra," "select," and "ordinary." The "extra" quality is produced exclusively from pericarp tissue (fruit walls). The "select" grade is prepared from the pericarp and seeds. The "ordinary" is prepared by grounding pericarp, seeds, and stems. Spanish paprika peppers have thicker, fleshier fruits.

Spanish Pimenton (or smoked paprika) is created by slowly drying the red peppers over a slow burning oak fire, a process that takes about two weeks. Being rotated daily during this drying process gives the Pimenton its distinctive smoky flavor. The variety of paprika grown will determine the heat level of the Pimenton, from dulce to picante. Smoked paprika is delicious in everything from potato dishes to eggs and pretty much any meat.

In the Teaching Garden, you can find examples of all three types of paprika. NuMex Garnet is an example of a United States paprika, Hungarian Yellow Wax is a Hungarian paprika, and Bola is a Spanish paprika.

Experiment with the different paprika peppers to find the one you like best. Also, experiment with smoked paprika: our favorite preparation is to harvest red paprika and smoke it over pecan wood.

(Opposite page)
Hungarian Paprika
Tomato Pepper.

INGREDIENTS

1 lb. lean pork tenderloin

1 tbsp. olive oil

3 tbsps. Hungarian paprika powder

¼ tsp. cayenne pepper

One 15–oz. can tomato sauce

1¼ cups water

1 red and 1 yellow bell pepper (deveined, deseeded, roasted, and cut into 1–inch pieces)

Cracked black pepper to taste

2 cups cooked medium grain brown rice

Salt to taste

Hungarian Goulash

Hungarian goulash is flavorful and easy to prepare. Cayenne pepper adds a little surprise "kick" and the sweet bell peppers bring it all together. Be sure to test the heat of your Hungarian paprika before adding it to the other ingredients.

INSTRUCTIONS

Cut the pork into 1-inch pieces. Bring the olive oil to medium high heat in a medium skillet. Add the pork (with a pinch of salt, if desired) and cook until browned on all sides—about 5 minutes. Add the paprika, cayenne pepper, tomato sauce, and water. Bring to a boil, reduce the heat; cover and simmer gently for 30 minutes. Be careful to keep the simmering temperature low after adding the Hungarian paprika because it can develop a bitter taste if heated too long. Add the bell peppers and cook an additional 10 to 15 minutes until the meat is tender and peppers are soft. Serve over rice with cracked black pepper. Serves 4.

Hungarian Lesco

Lesco is a vegetable stew that combines three of Hungary's favorite ingredients—peppers, tomatoes, and Hungarian paprika. It can be eaten on its own like a hardy vegetable stew, served over rice or potatoes, or used as a sauce for any kind of meat or pasta.

INSTRUCTIONS

Cover the bottom of a medium soup pot or a large deep skillet in olive oil and heat over medium heat. Sauté the onions in the oil until they just start to get a few brown bits. Add the garlic and sauté for about 30 seconds, or until it becomes very fragrant. Pull the pot off the heat and stir in the ground paprika and salt and pepper to taste. If you don't pull the pot off the heat, the paprika will likely burn, creating a bitter taste. Once the spices are mixed with the juices in the pot, return it to the heat. Mix in the optional vegetables for a flavor boost and sauté for about 30 seconds, stirring constantly so it doesn't burn. Add the tomatoes, bell peppers, and about ½ cup of water. Stir, then cover. Cook until the veggies are tender—10 to 30 minutes. Give your lecso a taste and adjust for salt, pepper, and ground paprika. If you find the consistency a little thin, cook for a few more minutes with the lid off to allow for evaporation. If it's a little thick, add in a bit more water and stir well. Garnish with parsley. Serves 4.

INGREDIENTS

Olive oil

2 large onions (diced)

2 or 3 garlic cloves (chopped)

1 tbsp. Hungarian ground paprika

Salt and pepper

5 or 6 large tomatoes (chopped)

3 bell peppers (chopped)

½ cup water

Fresh parsley for garnish

OPTIONAL FLAVOR BOOSTS

½ carrot (chopped)

½ parsnip (chopped)

4 to 5 cherry tomatoes (sliced in half)

½ bunch fresh parsley (chopped)

Ancho/Poblano, Mulato, and Pasilla

The ancho, mulato, and pasilla peppers are known as the holy trinity because of their use in moles. There is a lot of confusion about the chile pepper known as ancho, which is often called "poblano," at least in the United States. The produce industry uses the name for any green ancho fruit, but technically "poblano" reflects a specific ancho grown in the region of Puebla, Mexico. The Teaching Garden demonstrates the differences.

ANCHO/POBLANO

Ancho means wide in Spanish, alluding to the heart-shaped, thin-walled pods in their dried form. Anchos have been a favorite in both Mexico and the Southwest for centuries and are commonly stocked in grocery store produce departments. Anchos have a moderately rapid mild heat that dissipates quickly. They are often roasted and peeled, then preserved by canning or freezing. Anchos have a distinct sweet and fruity flavor. Roasting gives the pods an earthy, smoky flavor. Fresh anchos are often stuffed to make chile rellenos

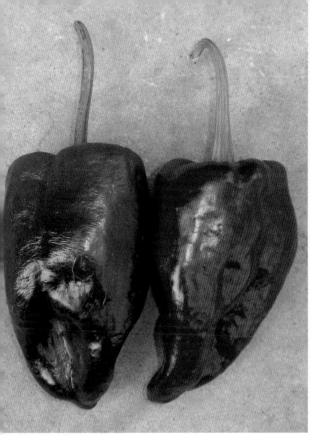

Green (poblano) and mature red Ancho fruits.

(stuffed peppers). Dried ancho pods can be stored in airtight containers for months. To rehydrate, place pieces in warm water for one to two hours.

Anchos are a staple in traditional Mexican dishes, such as mole sauce and tamales. Mole is the most beloved sauce of Mexico, and each mole recipe is as diverse as the chef that prepares it. Moles do not overpower with heat; rather, they do so with a complexity of flavors. They are made to be savored. The term *mole* is a derivation from the word *molli*, which means "concoction" or "mixture" in the Nahuatl language of the Aztec in Mesoamerica.

Skirt Steak with Chile Apple Relish

INGREDIENTS

1 tbsp. coffee (finely ground)

1 tbsp. ancho chile powder

2 tsps. kosher salt

1½ tsps. brown sugar

1½ to 2 lbs. skirt steak

¼ lb. mild green chiles, such as poblanos (deveined, deseeded, and cut in half)

½ Granny Smith apple (quartered and cored)

½ small yellow onion (cut into thick slices)

1 tbsp. vegetable oil

Salt and pepper

½ tsp. oregano leaves (chopped)

½ tsp. lime juice

Aluminum foil

It's an unusual combination, but when coffee and chile mingle with meat, the flavor is extraordinary. The relish adds an exclamation point!

INSTRUCTIONS

Heat a grill to medium high (350°F to 450°F). In a small bowl, combine the coffee, chile powder, salt, and brown sugar. Rub all over the steak and let it sit for at least 10 minutes. Combine the green chiles, apple, and onion with the oil and season to taste with salt and pepper. Grill the steak, turning once (dry rub on the meat will be very dark), 8 to 10 minutes total for medium-rare. Meanwhile, place a piece of aluminum foil on the grill and lay the chiles, apple, and onion on the foil and grill until lightly charred all over, 6 to 8 minutes. Transfer everything to a cutting board, tent the steak with foil, and let rest for 5 minutes. Next, chop the chiles, apple, and onion and transfer to a medium bowl. Stir in the oregano and lime juice and season to taste with salt and pepper. Thinly slice the steak against the grain and top with chile apple relish.

Ancho-Orange Hot Fudge

Once children try this rich, deep, and flavorful combination, they may never go back to plain hot fudge.

INSTRUCTIONS

Place the butter, corn syrup, brown sugar, cocoa powder, and chocolate in a medium saucepan. Cook over medium to low heat until the chocolate is fully melted, stirring constantly. Stir in the evaporated milk, bring to a boil, and continue to cook until the sauce thickens, about 5 to 10 minutes, stirring occasionally. Remove from the heat and add in the vanilla, chile powder, and orange extract; stir to combine. Season with salt to taste. Let the sauce cool until warm, then serve over vanilla ice cream or store in an airtight container in the refrigerator for up to a week, reheating before use. Makes 2 cups.

INGREDIENTS

8 tbsps. butter

½ cup light corn syrup

⅓ cup dark brown sugar

¼ cup unsweetened cocoa powder

4 oz. semisweet chocolate (finely chopped)

One 12–oz. can evaporated milk

1 tsp. vanilla extract

1 tsp. ancho red chile powder

½ tsp. orange extract

Kosher or sea salt

Vanilla ice cream

POBLANO

Poblanos, technically speaking, are anchos originating from the state of Puebla in central Mexico. They have thick, dark-green skin and a wide base that tapers to a point. They are mild to medium hot, registering between 1,000 and 2,000 SHUs. When dried, the poblano is called ancho. They're sometimes smoked as well. Sometimes you'll see smoked poblanos erroneously referred to as chipotles. But the word ancho refers to dried poblanos, smoked or not, while chipotle is meant to refer to dried and smoked jalapeno pepper. Poblanos are good candidates for roasting, which brings out the fruitier flavors and facilitates skin removal.

(Opposite page)
Poblano peppers.
Image courtesy of
Garrett Heath, licensed
under CC by 2.0.

Stuffed Poblanos

Use fresh poblanos or ancho chile peppers (depending on which name is used at your market). Remember that the heat can range from mild to hot, so if your dish turns out to be too warm for your dinner table, use sour cream to cool palates.

INSTRUCTIONS

Turn oven broiler on. When hot, place the poblanos on a foil-lined baking sheet. Broil 3 inches from the heat for 12 minutes or until blackened, turning over at 6 minutes. Put the peppers in a paper bag and fold the bag to close it tightly. Let the bag stand for 15 minutes. Once the peppers are cool enough to handle, put on plastic gloves. Run the peppers under cool water and peel, discarding the skins. Cut a lengthwise slit in each pepper. Scrap out and discard the veins and seeds. Set aside. Place the ancho chiles in a bowl. Cover with boiling water and let stand for 10 minutes to rehydrate. Drain water. Reset oven to 400°F. Heat a large frying pan covering the bottom of the pan with a thin layer of cooking spray and turn stove on to medium heat. Add the onions and garlic. Cook for at least 4 minutes or until crisp. Split the onion-garlic mixture in half and set half of it aside. Add ½ teaspoon salt, black pepper, and beef to the one-half mixture remaining in

INGREDIENTS

8 large poblano peppers

4 dried ancho chile peppers

3 cups yellow onion (chopped)

10 garlic cloves (minced)

1 tsp. salt

1 tsp. black pepper

12 oz. lean ground sirloin

4 oz. cream cheese (softened)

2 cups rice (precooked)

1½ cups queso fresco (crumbled)

¼ cup fresh lime juice

1 tbsp. ground cumin

2 tsps. sugar

2 14.5-oz. cans unsalted diced tomatoes (undrained)

Sour cream (optional)

Aluminum foil

Cooking spray

the frying pan. Cook until beef is done, stirring to crumble. Remove from the heat. Add the cream cheese, stirring until well combined. Stir in precooked rice and ¾ cup of queso fresco. Place the ancho chiles, reserved onion-garlic mixture, lime juice, cumin, sugar, tomatoes, and ½ teaspoon salt in a blender until smooth. Coat an 11-inch x 17-inch glass or ceramic baking dish with cooking spray. Pour 2 cups of sauce into the bottom of the dish. Open the poblano chiles, flattening each one slightly, and lay them into the dish, spacing them evenly. Divide beef mixture among chiles. Top evenly with remaining sauce and queso. Bake at 400° for 20 minutes or until bubbly. Allow to cool for 10 minutes before serving. Top with sour cream, as desired. Serves 4 to 8.

INGREDIENTS

2 poblano chile peppers

8 oz. elbow pasta

2 tbsps. unsalted butter

4 garlic cloves (minced)

2 tbsps. all-purpose flour

1½ cups whole milk

1 tsp. mustard powder

¼ tsp. cayenne powder

½ tsp. ground cumin

1 tsp. lime zest

½ cup cilantro (chopped)

Salt and pepper to taste

4 cups white cheddar (grated)

½ cup cotija cheese

Macaroni and Cheese

This recipe is packed with the flavors of roasted poblano peppers, cheese, and a hint of lime.

INSTRUCTIONS

Roast the poblano peppers under the broiler or on a grill until blackened, about 3 to 5 minutes per side. Place the roasted peppers in a paper sack, close tightly, and let sit for 20 minutes. Remove the peppers from the bag, run under faucet water and rub off the skin. Remove the stem and seeds and chop the chile peppers into 1-inch-long pieces. Bring a large pot of salted water to a boil and add the pasta. Cook according to package instructions but not to the point that the pasta is mushy—about 5 minutes. Drain the pasta. Preheat the oven to 375°F. Grease a large baking dish or a large 12-inch cast-iron skillet. Pour the drained pasta into the dish or skillet. In a separate pot, melt the butter on low heat. Add the garlic and cook for 1 minute. Whisk in the flour and cook until a light brown, toasty paste is formed, about 1 minute. Whisk in the milk and stir until it's thickened a bit but still fluid, about 1 to 2 minutes. Remove the pot from the heat and stir in the mustard powder, cayenne, cumin, lime zest, cilantro, and chopped poblano peppers. Adjust the seasoning and add salt and pepper, as desired.

Slowly add half of the cheddar cheese and stir until it's melted and well combined into the sauce. If needed, return the pot to low heat to completely blend. If the sauce gets too thick, you can thin it by stirring in a little milk, a teaspoon at a time. Pour sauce over pasta and top with the remaining half of the cheddar cheese and bake uncovered for 20 minutes or until brown and bubbling. Sprinkle with cotija cheese and serve immediately. Serves 4.

MULATO

If an ancho fruit matures to a dark brown color, the chile pepper is known as mulato. The fruit flavor becomes distinctly different from that of ancho or poblano chile. Mulatos have a complex flavor that has been described as chocolatey, smoky, or licorice-tasting, with hints of cherry, coffee, raisins, and tobacco. The mulato's moderate heat allows for flavor in a dish without concern for adding too much heat. The extra ripening adds more to a mulato's flavor, making a subtle difference but one that has its place in Mexican cuisine. Mulatos are the hottest member of the "holy trinity."

Chicken with Mulato Chile Sauce

The mulato chile peppers in this dish have a smoky-sweet aromatic quality that makes them terrific with Beaujolais wine.

INSTRUCTIONS

Put the mulato chiles in a medium bowl and cover with the hot water and hold them under water with an inverted small plate. Let the chiles soak until softened, about 30 minutes. Drain the chiles, reserving ½ cup of the soaking liquid. Destem, deseed, and coarsely chop the chiles. Heat a large nonstick skillet. Season the chicken with salt and pepper and add the pieces to the skillet, skin side down. Cover partially and cook over moderately high heat until well-browned on both sides, about 15 minutes. Transfer the chicken to a plate. Pour off all but 1 tbsp. of fat from the skillet. Add the scallions, garlic, onion, and chorizo to the remaining fat in the skillet and cook, stirring, until softened, about 4 minutes. Add the chopped chiles, wine, tomato, oregano, and the reserved ½ cup of chile soaking liquid and simmer for 1 minute. Arrange the chicken in the skillet, skin side up. Tuck the chayote in between the pieces of chicken. Cover and cook over low heat until the chayote is tender and the chicken is cooked through, about 30 minutes. Transfer the chicken and chayote to plates. Boil the sauce over high heat until reduced, about 4 minutes. Season with salt and pepper. Spoon the sauce around the chicken and serve with achiote rice. Serves 4.

INGREDIENTS

2 large dried mulato chile peppers

3 cups hot water

4 chicken drumsticks

4 chicken thighs

Salt and pepper

3 large scallions (coarsely chopped)

2 large garlic cloves (coarsely chopped)

1 medium onion (coarsely chopped)

1 oz. firm chorizo (cut into ½-inch diced pieces)

¼ cup dry white wine

1 large tomato (cut into 1-inch diced pieces)

1 tsp. dried oregano

2 small chayote (peeled, quartered lengthwise and pitted)

3 cups achiote rice (cooked)

INGREDIENTS

4 cups cold water

¾ cup black beans

1 tsp. and 2 tbsps. olive oil

¾ lb. beef short rib (cut apart)

2 dried pasilla chiles

1 large onion (diced and divided)

1 large carrot (peeled and diced)

12 tomatillos (peeled)

4 medium plum tomatoes *or* one 12–oz. can tomatoes (diced)

8 garlic cloves (chopped)

2 tsps. ground cumin

1 tsp. black pepper

1 tsp. oregano

3 cups rice (cooked)

Latin-Style Short Ribs

The adobo sauce is Guatemalan and is a traditional ingredient in Latin soups and stews. Tomatoes and tomatillos are the base of the sauce. When combined with the pasilla chile peppers and flavorful spices, it becomes a tangy sauce perfect for slow-cooked beef short ribs.

INSTRUCTIONS

Combine the cold water and dry black beans into a large bowl and soak them overnight. Drain and rinse before using. In a large Dutch oven, heat 1 tsp. of olive oil to medium heat. Add the short ribs and sear for 4 to 5 minutes, moving them in the pot so that they sear completely on all sides. Remove the beef and keep warm. Remove the stems and seeds from the dried pasillas and tear the chiles into pieces. Add the pasilla chiles, ½ of the onions, the diced carrots, tomatillos, tomatoes, and about 2 cups of water to a Dutch oven and simmer at a gentle boil for about 10 minutes. Drain and put the mixture in a blender or food processor with the other ½ of the onion, all the garlic, cumin, black pepper, oregano, and remaining 2 tablespoons of olive oil. Process to a thick puree. Strain the sauce through a sieve over a bowl, pushing down on the solids with the back of a spoon. Discard solids. Add the short ribs and sauce back to the Dutch oven and add just enough water to cover the meat. Turn the heat to low and cook, partially covered, for 1½ to 2 hours. Stir occasionally and add water if the sauce gets too thick. Meat will be tender and fall off the bone when ready. Serve over rice. Serves 4.

PASILLA

Pasillas are included in this section because, like anchos, poblanos, and mulatos, the pasilla is commonly used in mole recipes. In Spanish, *pasilla* means "raisin" (referring to its wrinkled fruit, with a raisin or coffee flavor), and many dried, wrinkled chile peppers are mistaken for pasillas, creating even more confusion. However, a pasilla is a very different chile from its dried, wrinkled cousins. It is long, cylindrical, and skinny, beginning as a dark green pod and maturing to a rich brown. The pasilla fruit is undulating, with each pod measuring 6 to 12 inches in length and 1 to 2 inches in width. The dark green pasilla fruit is called "chilaca" in the Mexican marketplace and is used like green peppers are in the United States—chopped and sprinkled in fresh salads.

Capsicum annuum

INGREDIENTS

8 dried mulato chile peppers (deveined and deseeded)

1 dried ancho chile pepper (deveined and deseeded)

6 dried pasilla chile peppers (deveined and deseeded)

Roma tomatoes (cut into quarters)

1 tomatillo (husked and quartered)

1 medium onion (halved)

1 garlic clove (unpeeled)

5 tbsps. vegetable oil or lard

10 whole black pepper–corns

5 garlic cloves (diced)

1 stick cinnamon

½ tsp. whole coriander seeds

½ tsp. whole anise seeds

(continued on next page)

Oaxacan Mole Sauce

Mole sauces are considered the cornerstone of the Mexican cuisine, with Oaxaca often called the "Land of Seven Moles." This recipe originates from the Oaxacan region. Use the mole sauce as a topping over your choice of beef or poultry.

INSTRUCTIONS

In a frying skillet, under a preheated broiler or on a barbeque grill, dry roast the already dry mulato, ancho, and pasillas, flipping occasionally, until they start to blister and change color. Transfer the chile peppers to a bowl of hot water and soak for 15 minutes. Drain the peppers and reserve the water. Transfer the peppers into a blender and blend until smooth, adding the reserved water, as needed. Push the puree through a mesh sieve and set aside. Dry roast the tomatoes, tomatillos, onion, and garlic in a frying skillet over moderate heat. Remove from the heat and let cool. Once cool enough to handle, peel the tomatoes and the garlic. Heat 1 tablespoon of the lard in a small skillet, over moderately low heat. Add the peppercorns, cloves, cinnamon, coriander, and anise seeds and toast until fragrant. Remove from the heat. Using the remaining 4 tbsp. of lard, fry the raisins until they are plump and change color. Remove with a slotted spoon. Continue the frying process with the almonds, pumpkin seeds, sesame seeds, tortillas, bread, and reserved chile, adding more lard if needed. In a blender or food processor, puree the roasted vegetables, spices, and fried ingredients in small batches, adding water, as needed, to form a smooth puree. Strain through a fine-mesh sieve and set aside. In a Dutch oven over moderate heat, heat the canola oil until hot but not smoking. Fry the chile puree, stirring constantly until it changes color, about 8 minutes. Add the reserved vegetable and spice mixture. Reduce the heat and simmer, stirring occasionally until the mole thickens, about 1 hour. Add about 2 cups of the reserved broth and simmer for 30 minutes. The mole should be thick enough to coat the back of a spoon. Add the chocolate and cook for 10 to 12 minutes. Season to taste with salt and sugar and add more chocolate, if needed. To serve, ladle mole over the chicken until it is completely covered, then garnish with toasted sesame seeds. Serves 4.

5 tsps. black raisins

20 whole blanched almonds

2 oz. pumpkin seeds

½ cup sesame seeds

2 stale corn tortillas

3 stale baguettes (cut into 1–inch slices)

1 tbsp. canola oil

2 cups beef or chicken broth

4 oz. Mexican chocolate or more to taste (coarsely chopped)

1 tsp. kosher salt

Up to ½ cup of sugar, as needed

¼ cup sesame seeds (lightly toasted) for garnish

INGREDIENTS

1 tbsp. olive oil

1 small yellow onion (diced)

1 garlic clove (minced)

1 tsp. ground cumin

One 15-oz. can black beans (drained and rinsed)

2 pasilla fresh chile peppers

½ tsp. brown sugar

Four 8-inch whole-wheat flour tortillas

½ cup Mexican cheese (grated)

2 cups shredded cabbage or lettuce

Juice from 1 lime

Cilantro

1 cup tomatoes (diced)

Oaxacan Tlayuda (Mexican Pizza)

This is considered a classic street food in Oaxaca, Mexico. Just like an American pizza, a variety of ingredients can be added beyond, or used in place of, what is suggested here. The pasilla chile added to the black bean puree gives this dish its heat and smoky flavor.

INSTRUCTIONS

Preheat oven to 450°F or grill to medium high heat. In a small skillet, heat the oil to medium high heat and add the onion, cooking for about 5 minutes until translucent. Add the garlic and cumin, cooking for 1 more minute to combine flavors. In a food processor, add the beans, onion mixture, pasilla chile, brown sugar, and about 3 tablespoons water. Blend until smooth. Add salt and pepper to taste. Lay the tortillas on a baking sheet or on aluminum foil on the grill, being careful not to overlap tortillas and using 2 baking sheets, as needed. Spread the bean mixture and cheese on tortillas and bake 5 to 7 minutes in the oven or on the grill until edges of the tortillas become crisp and brown. Combine the cabbage, lime juice, and cilantro for a slaw topping. Cut into triangles and serve with slaw and tomatoes. Serve warm. Serves 4.

CAYENNE

Cayenne is another unique group of chile peppers, which come in different shapes and sizes but are all very hot. The origin of the cayenne pepper is unknown; however, we do know that it is named after the Cayenne River in French Guiana and is typically not grown in South America. Some speculate that the Portuguese may have transferred it to Europe, then into Africa and India, where it appears today in many forms. For the most part, cayenne pods are pendant, long, and slender, measuring up to 10 inches long and 1 inch wide. They are often wrinkled and irregular in shape. The young pods of cayenne can be green, light green, or yellow, depending on the cultivar, but all mature to red. The cayenne is very hot but is a versatile choice for the home gardener seeking a spicy, prolific chile pepper because a mature plant can easily produce up to forty pods. Cayenne is grown commercially in New Mexico, Louisiana, and Texas, Africa, India, Japan, and Mexico. Pods can be eaten fresh in their immature green form in salsa, but the most common use is to grind the dried red pods into powder or flakes.

   In the United States, cayenne pepper is used fresh, dried, or chopped fresh and mixed with about 20 percent salt and then allowed to ferment. The resulting "mash" is the key ingredient in Louisiana-style hot sauces like Frank's Red Hot, Louisiana Hot Sauce, and Texas Pete. In the United States, New Mexico leads in commercial production of cayenne for hot sauces, with two large processing facilities located in Las Cruces. Retail sales of hot sauces

(Opposite page)
NuMex Las Cruces
cayenne fruits.

reached more than $2.71 billion in 2021 and have been estimated to grow to $4.38 billion in 2028.

Red pepper flakes are found in every pizzeria across America: most of the time, these are dried cayenne chile peppers. The crushed cayenne pepper is not only perfect for sprinkling on top of pizza but can be used as an ingredient in pasta dishes and for infusing olive oil, chili, soups, and stews.

INGREDIENTS

Dough

1 cup soft margarine or butter

1½ cups sugar

2 large eggs

2¾ cups flour

2 tsps. cream of tartar

1 tsp. baking soda

½ tsp. salt

Spice Mix Topping (enough to make two batches of cookies)

1 tbsp. fennel seeds

8 whole pepper cloves

20 black peppercorns

½ tsp. ground dry ginger

½ tsp. ground cumin

1 tsp. ground coriander

½ tsp. ground cardamom

1 tsp. ground cinnamon

¼ tsp. cayenne powder

1 pinch salt

¼ cup sugar

Sparkler Doodles

Try this fun recipe with your kids as an afterschool snack. You can also serve the doodles with a dish of ice cream following a meal of chicken mole.

INSTRUCTIONS

Cream the margarine or butter with the sugar. Add the eggs and mix well. Sift together the flour, cream of tartar, baking soda, and salt and add to creamed mixture. Mix well. Chill the dough for at least an hour. While the dough is chilling, make the spice mix. Place the fennel seeds, cloves, and peppercorns in a coffee grinder and grind to a fine powder. Add the rest of the spices and salt to the ground spices and mix well. Mix 5 teaspoons of the spice mix with ¼ cup sugar. Preheat the oven to 400°F. Roll the chilled dough into balls the size of a small walnut. Roll the balls in the spice and sugar mix, coating evenly. Place the coated balls about 2 inches apart on an ungreased cookie sheet. Bake for 5 to 10 minutes or until lightly browned and the centers of the cookies are just beginning to flatten. Remove from the cookie sheet immediately. Yields 24.

Pineapple, Mango, and Passion Fruit Granita

Granita is a semifrozen dessert originating in Sicily. It is considered a cousin to sorbet and Italian ice but with a coarser, crystalline texture. Try it as a patio dessert on a hot summer evening.

INSTRUCTIONS

In a medium saucepan, bring the water and sugar to a boil, stirring until the sugar is completely dissolved. Cool completely. In a blender, puree the pineapple, mango, and ¼ cup plus 2 tbsp. of the sugar water. Once pureed, stir in the passion fruit juice and cayenne, as well as the remainder of the sugar water. Transfer the fruit mixture to a shallow rectangular dish and place in the freezer. Stir with a fork to break up the ice crystals every hour until firm (about 5 hours). Just before serving, scrape the granita with a fork to create a fluffy texture. Serve in small ice cream dishes. Garnish with a sprig of basil, if desired. Serves 6 to 8.

INGREDIENTS

½ cup water

½ cup sugar

2 cups fresh pineapple (cut into bite–sized chunks)

1 cup fresh mango (cut into bite–sized chunks)

4 cups passion fruit juice (chilled)

½ tsp. cayenne powder

Sprig basil (optional)

Chilhuacle Amarillo, Rojo, and Negro

Chilhuacle is a rare, endemic landrace grown in southern Mexico around Oaxaca, primarily in the Cañada Valley, a designated UNESCO ecological zone. The name suggests domestication was pre-Columbian because *chilhuacle* means "ancient chile" in Nahuatl, the language of the Aztecs. Chilhuacle pods vary in shape but usually measure from 3 to 5 inches in length and from 2 to 2½ inches in width. The fruits are thin-walled, with some looking like miniature bell peppers while others are broad shouldered and tapering to a point. Immature fruits are green, ripening to yellow, red, or black; hence the names Chilhuacle Amarillo (yellow), Chilhuacle Rojo (red), and Chilhuacle Negro (black). They provide a deep, intense flavor that is unique to mole sauces, for which Oaxaca is famous. Chilhuacle Negro is a chile with strong notes of cocoa, tobacco, dry fruit; moderately hot, this chile pepper is the cornerstone of authentic Oaxacan mole recipes. Chilhuacle Rojo is typically used in making mole coloradito. Both "rojo" and "coloradito" mean various shades of the color red. Chilhuacle

(Opposite page) Chilhuacle yellow, even though it looks orange to us.

Amarillo is the key ingredient in mole amarillo, one of the seven major Oaxacan moles. The dried pods can be ground into powder to provide a wonderful heat source for seasoning any dish. Most commonly they are crushed and added to soups, stews, and bean dishes. Green fruit is chopped and used in salsas or to produce a chile pepper vinegar. Heat levels are between 50,000 to 100,000 SHUs.

Mole is rooted in pre-Hispanic Indigenous traditions. The culinary use of chilhuacle chile peppers in the Oaxacan regional cuisine has been recognized as a component of Mexican cuisine by the Intangible Cultural Heritage of Humanity for the Organization of the United Nations for Education, Sciences and Culture (UNESCO), which emphasizes the importance of this crop. Despite its importance in Oaxacan cuisine and the demand for it, chilhuacle chile pepper is a variety that is increasingly less cultivated and is in danger of extinction.

A mole amarillo is often served with chicken, chayote, potatoes, and green beans. It is also delicious with grilled fish and mussels. Mole amarillo is by far the most beautiful of all the moles. The flavor is very light and intensely spicy, but what is more amazing is the intense color!

INGREDIENTS

4 tbsps. butter

1 whole chicken (cut into pieces)

1 red tomato (cut into pieces)

8 green tomatoes *or* tomatillos (husks removed and sliced into quarters)

2 Chilhuacle Amarillo, Rojo, *or* Negro chiles (destemmed)

2 guajillos chiles (destemmed)

1 yellow onion (coarsely chopped)

2 cups water

4 garlic cloves (roasted)

2 garlic cloves (chopped)

½ tsp. allspice

3 peppercorns

½ cup masa corn flour

1 tbsp. oil

1 sprig epazote

1 bunch parsley

Slightly roasted leaves of hoja santa

Salt

Cooked white rice as side dish

Yellow Mole Chicken

This is one of the easier moles to make but sourcing a couple of the ingredients might be tricky. It gets its name from the Chilhuacle Amarillo pepper and, like every mole recipe, is an exquisite combination of spicy and sweet flavors.

INSTRUCTIONS

In a large skillet, melt 2 tablespoons of butter and fry the chicken pieces for a few minutes, until about half cooked. Roast the tomatoes, tomatillos, four garlic cloves, chiles, and onion in the oven, to the point where they are starting to char, but do not burn them. Add 1 cup water to the blender and blend the remaining two garlic cloves, allspice, peppercorns, roasted green tomatoes, roasted red tomatoes, and chiles. Pour this mixture with the fried chicken and add 1 more cup of water and the masa corn flour, gently mixing until smooth. Add salt, if desired. Simmer 40 minutes. Just before serving, blend the epazote, parsley, and hoja santa with a little water in a food processor. Simmer 5 more minutes with the new ingredients and turn off the heat. The mole amarillo should have the consistency of heavy cream. Serves 6.

Chayote (Squash) with Amarillo Pepper

Make this delightful side dish a couple times and you'll soon be making it from memory.

1 tbsp. butter

2 chayote (chopped)

½ tsp. white sugar

4 garlic cloves (chopped)

1 tsp. amarillo pepper flakes

1 tsp. fresh ginger (chopped)

Salt and ground black pepper to taste

INSTRUCTIONS

Melt the butter in a skillet heated over medium heat. Next, stir the chayote, sugar, garlic, pepper flakes, and ginger into the butter. Cook, stirring frequently until the chayote are tender, about 15 minutes. Season with salt and black pepper. Serve within 30 minutes of preparing. Serves 2 to 3.

Costeno and Costeno Amarillo

Costenos add fruit overtones to salsas, sauces, and soups. Two varieties, Costeno and Costeno Amarillo, are both from the Oaxaca and Guerrero regions of Mexico. Both have pods that begin as green.

Costeno pods mature to a red-orange. They taper to a point and measure about 2 to 3 inches long and ½ to ¾ inch at the shoulder. The pod has thin-to-medium-fleshed walls and an apricot fruit tone, with a fiery, intense, lingering heat.

Costeno Amarillo is shiny and amber in color, tapering to a point and measuring about 2 to 3 inches long and ¾ to 1 inch across at the shoulders. The pods have very thin flesh with a light, crisp lemon-citrus flavor and green tomato and grassy tones. The heat is lower when compared to Costeno and has an added subtlety. Dried pods are used to prepare yellow mole sauces and are also good in soups and stews. The dried pods are ground without seeds to season mole sauces. If the seeds do remain after grinding, the pod tends to have a nutty flavor.

INGREDIENTS

1 tsp. olive oil

1 medium yellow onion (peeled and chopped)

2 tbsps. garlic (minced)

8 cups salt–free chicken broth *or* vegetable stock

one 14.5–oz can diced tomatoes (undrained)

¼ cup lime juice

2 fresh Costeno Amarillo chile peppers (deveined, deseeded, and finely chopped)

1 jalapeno pepper (deveined, deseeded, and thinly sliced)

Six 6–inch corn tortillas

½ cup fresh cilantro (chopped)

Cooking spray

Salsa Soup

This soup is one of those great last-minute dishes when you want something flavorful but don't have a lot of time to prepare a meal.

INSTRUCTIONS

Heat the oil to medium high in a large soup pot. Add the onion and cook until tender. Add the garlic, broth, tomatoes, lime juice, Costeno Amarillo chile peppers, and jalapeno pepper. Bring the soup to boiling and simmer 20 minutes. Preheat oven to 350°F. Place the tortillas on a baking sheet and lightly coat with cooking spray. Bake for 10 to 12 minutes until crisp and lightly browned. Remove from oven and let cool. Break the tortillas into chip-sized pieces. Stir the cilantro into the hot soup. Ladle the soup into bowls and top with baked tortilla chips. Serves 10 (1-cup bowls).

INGREDIENTS

6 Costeno Amarillo chile peppers (destemmed)

½ lb. tomatillos (husked)

1 garlic clove (chopped)

½ cup white onions (chopped)

⅓ cup fresh cilantro (chopped)

½ tsp. salt

Salsa Costena

This exciting salsa is bursting with flavor. If Costeno chile peppers are not available, try substituting de arbol peppers. This spicy salsa is great with fish, meat, or chicken or as a dip.

INSTRUCTIONS

In a medium iron skillet over medium high heat, cook the Costeno Amarillo chile peppers, stirring constantly, until dark brown. Do not allow the peppers to burn. Remove from heat and set aside. Place the tomatillos in a medium saucepan with enough water to cover. Bring to a boil. Cook 5 minutes, remove from the heat and drain. Place the chile peppers, tomatillos, and garlic in a blender or food processor. Blend until smooth. Transfer the chile pepper mixture to a medium bowl. Mix in the onions, cilantro, and salt. Chill in the refrigerator before serving. Yields 4 servings over a main dish.

De Arbol

The name *de arbol* means "of the tree" because most of this pepper's growth habit is treelike. A landrace chile pepper, the de arbol hails from the states of Jalisco and Nayarit, Mexico. Because its fruits retain their bright red color after drying, it is the chile pepper seen most often in dried pepper strings called ristras and decorative wreaths. De arbol or chile de arbol is narrow, curved, and a bit pointed at the tip or calyx, measuring less than ¼ inch wide at the tip and between 2 and 3 inches long with a thin flesh, which becomes translucent when dried. While growing they are green and mature to bright red. Tall plants (up to 4 feet) bear heavy loads of slender, curved peppers all summer long and are well adapted to most gardens. The plant can be spreading, so may benefit from staking. De arbol chile is very hot but loaded with a complex flavor profile often described as perfumy, smoky, and with oak notes. De arbol goes well in most chicken dishes.

(*Opposite page*)
NuMex Sunburst (orange), NuMex Sunglo (yellow), and NuMex Sunflare (red) de arbol chiles.

Pork (or Chicken) Tacos

Make "Taco Tuesday" authentic with this easy-to-follow taco recipe. Pork is marinated in a spicy chile sauce, for a delicious taco feast. But remember, chiles de arbol are very spicy. To make a milder recipe, cut down on the number of de arbol peppers and add more anchos— which are very mild.

INSTRUCTIONS

Place the pork pieces in a glass bowl and set aside. Bring a small pot of water to boil, add the dried chiles, tomato, garlic, and onion and simmer over low heat. Allow the chiles to rehydrate; the onion and tomato will take longer to soften. After the vegetables have soft-ened, remove the skin from the tomato. Place the soften onion, garlic, tomato, and chiles in a blender. Add a little salt, the vinegar, and blend until smooth. Taste and adjust seasoning, if desired. Pour the chile marinade over the pork, stir until well-combined and refrigerate overnight or for at least 30 minutes. While the meat is marinating chop up the toppings. The next day, or after 30 minutes, heat some oil and cook marinated pork until cooked through. Serve with corn tortillas, finely chopped onion and cilantro, lime or lemon wedges, and your favorite salsa. Yields 12 to 14 tacos.

INGREDIENTS

1½ lbs. boneless pork (cut into bite–sized pieces with excess fat removed)

1 dried ancho chile pepper

5 dried chiles de arbol

1 medium tomato

3 garlic cloves (minced)

1 medium onion (chopped)

Salt to taste

1 tbsp. apple cider vinegar (optional)

Olive oil *or* vegetable oil

Corn tortillas

Toppings

Onion (finely chopped)

Cilantro (chopped)

Lime *or* lemon wedges

Mexican cheese (grated)

Your favorite salsa

Capsicum annuum

Green Beans with Peanuts and Chile de Arbol

An inventive twist on casual green beans. After trying this recipe, you will not go back to a standard green bean recipe ever again.

INSTRUCTIONS

Bring salted water to a boil in a large pot, add the sliced green beans, and cook, uncovered, for 2 to 3 minutes; drain and set aside. Combine the soy sauce, chicken broth, sugar, and salt in a small bowl and mix well. Heat the peanut oil over high heat in a large heavy skillet until hot but not smoking. Add the peanuts, stirring constantly as they begin to fry, for about 20 seconds. Beware: peanuts burn faster than you would think so don't wait until they look browned. Add the garlic and the chiles de arbol, stirring for about 10 seconds. Add the scallions and stir for another 10 to 15 seconds. Add the green beans, stir to combine all the ingredients, and finally pour in the soy sauce mixture. Let all ingredients cook for 3 to 4 minutes. Serve immediately. Serves 4 to 6.

INGREDIENTS

1 lb. green beans (cut diagonally into 2–inch pieces)

1 tbsp. soy sauce

¼ cup chicken broth

½ tsp. brown sugar

½ sea salt

2 tbsps. peanut oil

½ cup roasted peanuts

4 garlic cloves (minced)

4 chiles de arbol (deveined and thinly sliced)

6 scallions (finely chopped)

Hungarian Wax

This chile originated in—surprise—Hungary! It couldn't have a more fitting name, but it does go by a few others. In Spanish, it is referred to as *güero*, which means light-skinned or blond. Sometimes it is simply known as the hot wax pepper or the hot yellow pepper. The other aspect of the name refers to the waxlike texture of the pepper's rind. This texture and the color (before ripening) make the Hungarian wax pepper look a lot like a banana pepper. But really that's about where the similarities stop. If you bite into a Hungarian wax pepper when expecting a banana pepper (500 SHUs), you're in for a spicy awakening: they average about 40,000 SHUs! Hot wax peppers do change color as they ripen, turning orange in hue, followed by red at full ripening. They're also large, topping out at 5 to 6 inches in length. And while they don't have the girth of a poblano pepper, they're not super-slim like a cayenne pepper, either. They've got a plumper shape, quite like a banana.

Some wax pepper varieties might remind you of those shiny plastic chile-shaped strings of holiday lights and in fact, those light strings can be purchased in the same bright colors (light yellow, bright-yellow, orange, orange-red, and red) that are typical of wax peppers. It's the waxy appearance of these peppers that gives them their common name.

Wax varietals come in lengths and pod shapes that vary from 2 to 8 inches in length. Caloro, Cascabella, Petite Sirah, Santa Fe Grande, and Floral Gem are short-fruited types. Sweet Banana, Ivory Banana, Hungarian Yellow Banana, Hot Banana, and Inferno are long-fruited. These prolific fruiting peppers produce early, typically in seventy days, and are an excellent container variety in difficult climates. Used fresh in salads, relishes, and as a garnish, they are best-known as "the pickled peppers," as they are the most common commercially pickled variety.

The cultivars can be either hot or not. The heat levels can vary greatly depending on the cultivar from the Banana Supreme, with no heat, to Inferno, which has a lot of heat. So, when one speaks about Hungarian wax peppers, they can range in flavor from mild and sweet to fiery hot.

(*Opposite page*) Basket of short–fruited yellow wax peppers.

Cheese-Stuffed Hungarian Wax Peppers

INGREDIENTS

15 Hungarian wax peppers

1 lb. dry curd cheese *or* farmer's cheese *or* ricotta

½ cup freshly grated Parmesan cheese

2 eggs (beaten)

1 tsp. salt

1 tsp. fresh parsley (chopped)

2 garlic cloves (minced)

1 tbsp. canola *or* vegetable oil

Cooking spray

This simple recipe can be served as either an appetizer or a main dish. When you have access to two or more of the varietals described above, you can accommodate even the most boastful chilehead in your group by identifying the heat levels (or not!) to your dinner guests.

INSTRUCTIONS

Heat your oven to 350°F. Line a baking pan with foil and lightly coat it with cooking spray. Cut off the tops of the peppers and set aside. Remove the seeds and veins of the peppers and toss. In a food processor, blend the dry curd cheese until smooth. Add the Parmesan cheese, eggs, salt, parsley, and garlic and mix well. Do not over-blend. Divide the cheese mixture evenly between each pepper, pushing it down to fill the pod. A piping bag will come in handy here, if you have one—the stuffing process can be a bit messy. Replace the tops. Place the stuffed peppers in your baking pans. Sprinkle with oil and bake for 35 to 45 minutes or until golden brown and cheese is melted and bubbly. Serves 6.

Hungarian Pasta Salad

Use as many fresh ingredients as you can for this salad. The combination of unique flavors and fresh peppers will have your guests asking for the recipe. You might want to have copies on hand!

INSTRUCTIONS

Wash the Hungarian peppers. Place on a cookie sheet and broil in the oven, watching closely and turning until the skin is black on both sides. Place the blackened peppers in a bowl, cover, and allow to cool for 10 to 15 minutes. In a second large salad bowl, combine the jalapenos, tomatoes, oregano, cilantro, onions, and garlic. Trim the corn kernels from the cobs with a sharp knife. When the red peppers are cool enough to handle, remove pepper skins, destem, and deseed. Cut the Hungarian peppers into small pieces and add to the large salad bowl of ingredients. Begin cooking pasta in boiling salted water according to package directions until al dente. Put the pumpkin seeds in a dry frying pan on medium heat and roast until fragrant (2 to 3 minutes). Remove seeds from the frying pan and set aside in a small bowl. Cook the corn kernels in the same dry frying pan, stirring constantly until brown spots appear (4 to 5 minutes). Allow to cool (5 minutes), then add the corn to the large salad

INGREDIENTS

8 to 10 red Hungarian wax peppers

2 jalapeno peppers (destemmed, deseeded, and finely chopped)

2 large tomatoes (remove seeds and chop into ½-inch cubes)

4 sprigs fresh oregano (finely cut leaves with kitchen shears and toss stems)

½ small bunch cilantro (finely cut leaves with kitchen shears and toss stems)

2 medium yellow onions (finely chopped)

2 garlic cloves (finely chopped)

3 ears corns

14 oz. penne (whole-grain)

Salt

4 tbsp. pumpkin seeds

5 tbsp. vegetable oil

1 tsp. cumin seeds

1 lime

Salt and pepper to taste

bowl. Place the oil in the frying pan. Add the onions and garlic and sauté until transparent (3 to 4 minutes). Add the cumin seeds to the onions and garlic. Cook for an additional 20 seconds. Add the onions, garlic, and cumin to large salad bowl and gently toss together. When the pasta is al dente, pour through a strainer, being careful to reserve 6 to 8 tablespoons of pasta water. Set pasta water aside in a small container. Mix pasta into salad ingredients, again tossing gently. Squeeze lime juice over salad, to taste. If the salad is a little dry, stir in a small amount of the pasta water. Season with salt and pepper, sprinkle with pumpkin seeds and serve. Serves 4.

Italian Frying

With a few steps in the Teaching Garden, one travels from Hungary to Italy. The Italian frying pepper is fun to grow and eat. No worries here about young ones picking them in the garden and being "stung" with heat. Mildness and flavorful are their middle names. With a zest just beyond the bell pepper, tons of juicy flavor, and a penchant for cooler climate habitation, it's a favorite among Italians and should be for you, too. Used in both the immature (green) state and the mature (red or yellow) state in Italian cooking, the diversity of this pepper is reflected in its fresh, crisp flesh. It is a favorite ingredient on pizzas and salads. It is excellent when sautéed in olive oil or stuffed and baked or grilled— all methods leaving the stems and seeds intact. The seeds give the peppers their characteristic fruity flavor and sweet taste. Also called Italianelles or Cubanelles, some popular varieties include Nardello, Italian Long, Pepperoncini, and Corno de Toro (red and yellow).

Chocolate Chip Cookies

Peppers and chocolate pair well together. Experiment with the amount and variety of chile peppers and chocolate used together in this recipe.

INSTRUCTIONS

Wash the chile pepper. Heat a nonstick skillet over medium heat and set whole chile in skillet. Cook the chile, turning frequently, until all sides are browned—about 5 minutes. Place in a paper bag and fold tightly closed. Allow to cool. When cooled, put on some plastic gloves and devein, deseed, and chop the pepper into fine pieces. Preheat oven to 350°F. In a medium-sized mixing bowl, whisk together the whole-wheat flour, all-purpose flour, wheat bran, baking soda, and salt. In a second mixing bowl, cream together the butter and the brown and white sugars. Be sure the mixer is on a low speed. Add the vanilla. Continue to mix, adding one egg at a time. Add the flour mixture into the butter mixture in batches until thoroughly combined. Stir in the chile pepper pieces and chocolate chips. Spray a cookie sheet with oil. Scoop out rounded teaspoons of cookie dough onto the cookie sheet. Space the balls 2 inches apart. Bake for 10 to 12 minutes or until cookies are lightly browned. Allow cookies to cool on the cookie sheet for 5 minutes before transferring to a cooling rack or plate. Yields 48.

INGREDIENTS

1 to 2 Italian frying peppers

1 ½ cups whole-wheat flour

1 cup all-purpose flour

½ cup wheat bran

½ tsp. baking soda

¾ tsp. salt

1 cup butter, unsalted, at room temperature

1 ½ cups brown sugar

½ cup granulated sugar

2 tsps. vanilla extract

2 large eggs

2 cups chocolate chips, semisweet

INGREDIENTS

6 large Italian peppers (deveined, deseeded, and chopped into 1-inch pieces)

⅓ cup extra virgin olive oil

2 garlic cloves (minced)

⅓ cup balsamic vinegar

Salt and pepper

⅓ cup fresh parsley (chopped)

Fried Sweet Peppers with Balsamic Vinegar

If you've harvested a few too many Italian peppers from the garden, this is the recipe for you. Use a good quality balsamic vinegar and the depth of flavor will turn your excess peppers into something special.

INSTRUCTIONS

Heat the oil in a large heavy skillet and add the peppers, stirring well to coat in the oil. Cook the peppers over medium heat until they begin to soften and brown, stirring often, for about 10 minutes. Add the garlic and cook another 1 to 2 minutes until fragrant. Add the balsamic vinegar, season with salt and pepper, and mix well. Cook another 3 to 4 minutes until the peppers have absorbed all of the vinegar. Toss with the fresh chopped parsley and place on a platter to serve as an appetizer or a side dish. Serves 4.

Jalapeno (Hot and Not)

In the Teaching Garden, there are several jalapenos bred by the NMSU breeding program. These include NuMex Jalmundo, NuMex Pinata, NuMex Primavera (winner of an IgNobel prize), and NuMex Vaquero. Named for the town of Jalapa, jalapenos are among the best-known chile peppers in the United States. This pepper produces 3-inch, thick-walled, moderately hot pods, with deep green color maturing to bright red. Widely adapted, jalapeno plants yield a bountiful harvest in dry or humid, hot or cool climates.

While most jalapenos are green, maturing to red, jalapenos of other colors have been developed. The cultivar plant has light green leaves and sets fruit prolifically. Widely adapted and early maturing, it can set fruit under most conditions, making it a great choice even in short-season areas. The thick-walled pods of NuMex Pinata make tasty salsa and sauces.

Most of the commercial jalapeno crop is canned or pickled. Often used on nacho chips, jalapenos are a main ingredient in salsas.

Jalapeno peppers have thick fruit walls, and the fruit skin may show netting, called corkiness, which is a desirable trait in Mexico but unfavorable in the United States. Corkiness does not affect the flavor.

(Opposite page) Jalapeno peppers. Image courtesy of Acton Crawford, licensed under CC by 2.0.

NuMex Jalmundo jalapeno fruits.

The thick skins keep pods from drying naturally on the plant. Mature red jalapenos are often dried by smoking them over a fire to make what is called "chipotle." The dried pods are then used as a dried smoky flavored spice. After smoking, they look like dried rumpled leather, but they add a rich, smoky, complex mixture of flavors to dishes, packing some heat (up to 50,000 SHUs). NuMex Pinata matures from light green to bright yellow to orange and finally to red as it ripens.

(Opposite page) NuMex Spice jalapenos.

INGREDIENTS

1½ cup stone ground cornmeal

½ cup all–purpose flour

¼ cup shortening

1½ cups nonfat butter–milk

2 tsps. baking powder

1 tsp. sugar

½ tsp. salt

½ tsp. baking soda

3 egg whites

1 each NuMex Lemon Spice, Orange Spice, and Pumpkin Spice pods (diced)

Cooking spray

Enchanted Chile Cornbread

While delicious just as it is, this recipe can also accommodate all kinds of personal touches. Feel free to add cheese, green onions, corn kernels, jalapeno peppers, cooked sausage, or a combination of your own creation. The combined volume of your add-ins should measure not more than 1 cup.

INSTRUCTIONS

Heat oven to 450°F. Spray an 8- x 8- x 2-inch square pan with nonstick cooking spray. Mix all ingredients together, mixing vigorously for 30 seconds. Pour into pan. Bake 20 to 25 minutes or until golden brown. Serves 8.

Chipotle Albondigas

We offer this recipe to encourage you to try making chipotle from your garden jalapenos. Chipotle adds a nice smoky flavor and a little kick to albondigas (meatballs). Typically, chipotle is used to flavor soups, salsas, stews, sauces, and even the occasional dessert.

Chipotle is made from dried and smoked red jalapeno peppers. The wood heat gives the jalapenos their chipotle, smoked flavor (we use

INGREDIENTS

4 to 8 chipotle chiles (finely chopped)

2 small white onions (finely chopped)

5 tomatoes (peeled and finely chopped)

¼ cup carrots (finely chopped)

¼ cup celery (finely chopped)

1 cup beef broth

¼ cup plus 2 tbsps. cilantro (finely chopped)

1¼ tsps. salt

1 tsp. black pepper

1 lb. ground pork

1 lb. ground beef

½ cup breadcrumbs

½ cup milk

2 eggs

pecan wood in New Mexico). To make chipotle, place washed, halved (halving peppers speeds up drying time) or whole red jalapenos on a low grill for 2 to 3 hours or until completely dried, turning at least twice. Cool and store in an airtight container until ready to use. When ready, either soak the chipotle in hot water for an hour or more and then pat dry and chop into small pieces, or grind dry unsoaked pepper in a coffee grinder or with a mutate and pestle.

INSTRUCTIONS

Preheat oven to 350°F. In a saucepan, combine the chipotle, 1 of the chopped onions, all the tomatoes, carrots, celery, and broth along with ¼ cup cilantro, ¼ teaspoon salt, and ½ teaspoon black pepper. Cook uncovered over medium heat for 10 minutes. Reduce heat and simmer for another 30 minutes. While the sauce is simmering, combine the remaining ingredients, mixing well, and shape into meatballs. Bake the meatballs for 20 minutes in the oven. Remove meatballs, drain excess liquid, and place the meatballs into the simmering chipotle sauce. Simmer for another 20 minutes. Serves 8.

Pepperoncini

Pepperoncini is well-known as a salad bar chile pepper. There are two types of pepperoncini: Italian and Greek. Italian has dark green pods. Greek, also called Tuscan, is medium-to-light green when picked fresh but turns a yellowish green when brined for commercial use. The plants grow upright and set fruit well. After a crop is picked, the plant will begin to reset fruits, so expect to continue harvesting to maximize production. Pepperoncini are almost always pickled or canned and seldom eaten fresh. Californians now are also grilling the pods and adding them to vegetable dishes. The pepperoncini probably came to Italy in the early sixteenth century, after Columbus had taken samples from the New World to Europe in 1492. Like the tomato, the pepperoncini were first considered a decorative and possibly poisonous plant before being adopted into Italian cuisine. Pietro Andrea Mattioli first described pepperoncini in 1568 and mentioned how much hotter they were than other varieties of pepper from Asia. Pepperoncini were used in a cookbook recipe for the first time in 1694, by the Neapolitan cook Antonio Latini. In his recipe for salsa alla spagnola, chopped pepperoncini, tomatoes and some onions are combined with peppermint, salt, and oil, to be served as a relish. If you are a pickled pepper person, this Italian pepper is for you. Expect gratifyingly large crops of 5- to 6-inch-long thin, slightly wrinkled peppers.

Pepperoncini peppers. Image courtesy of Joi Ito, licensed under CC by 2.0

At first, the peppers are a pleasing light green; as the season progresses, their color shifts into bright red. Take your pick: you can harvest the sweet, thin-walled fruits in either the green or red stage, and you can enjoy them raw, pickled, or cooked.

INGREDIENTS

3 tbsps. butter

2 lbs. chicken (cut into thin strips)

1 tsp. salt

1 tsp. ground pepper

¼ cup garlic (diced)

½ white onion (diced)

½ cup chicken stock

½ cup sliced and jarred fire-roasted red peppers (cut into strips and drained)

1 cup heavy cream

½ cup parmesan cheese (grated)

1 tbsp. Italian seasoning

½ cup pepperoncini peppers (cut into rings)

Creamy Pepperoncini Chicken Tender Skillet

A delicious tangy dinner that is great over rice or pasta or on its own.

INSTRUCTIONS

In a large, heavy pan, melt the butter on medium high heat. Season the chicken with salt and pepper. Add to the pan. We suggest cooking the chicken in a few smaller batches to allow the space for the chicken pieces to brown nicely. Brown the chicken on all sides, turning every few minutes, for about 8 minutes. Remove the chicken from pan (it might not have fully reached 165°F internal temperature, which is fine). Add the garlic and onion to pan and allow to brown for about 5 minutes. Add the chicken stock and red peppers and reduce heat in half for another 5 minutes. Turn the heat off and slowly stir in the cream and parmesan, whisking vigorously as you add the cream. Slowly bring the heat back to medium high, add the Italian seasoning, pepperoncini, and chicken back to pan. Let the sauce reduce to half and bring the chicken's internal temperature fully to 165°F. Remove from the heat and serve over rice or pasta or on its own. Serves 4.

Pepperoncini Pot Roast

This spicy recipe literally has only four ingredients. Serve it with a baked potato or offer it with a fresh hoagie bun.

INSTRUCTIONS

Combine all ingredients together in a slow cooker. Be sure to include the pepperoncini juice. Cook on low heat for 6 to 8 hours or until the meat is falling apart. Serves 8 to 10.

INGREDIENTS

3 to 5 lbs. beef roast

One 16–oz. jar pepperoncini peppers with liquid

1 package of dry Italian salad dressing mix

1 package of brown gravy mix

Aleppo/ Urfa Biber

This chile pepper, also known as Halaby, brings us to the Middle East. The Aleppo chile pepper is named after the long-inhabited city along the Silk Road in northern Syria. It is also grown in Turkey. These peppers ripen to a burgundy color and are then semidried, deseeded, and crushed or coarsely ground. The pepper flakes are known in Turkey as *pul biber*. Although it is a common condiment, its use in the United States outside of Armenian, Syrian, and Turkish immigrant communities was rare until the twentieth century, when its popularity rose among the broader United States population. The Aleppo pepper has a moderate heat level of about 10,000 on the Scoville scale, with some fruitiness and mild, cumin-like undertones. Its flavor is similar to that of the ancho chile, but oilier and slightly salty because salt is often used in the drying process. It is mild, with its heat building slowly, with a fruity raisin-like flavor. It has also been described as having the flavor of "sweetness, roundness and perfume of the best kind of sundried tomatoes, but with a substantial kick behind."

Urfa biber (also known as isot pepper) is very similar to the Aleppo pepper and is cultivated in the Urfa region of Turkey. It is often described as having a smoky, "raisin-like" taste. Urfa biber ripens to a dark maroon on the plant. The fruits go through a two-part process, where they are sun-dried during the day and wrapped tightly at night. The night process is called "sweating" and works to infuse the dried flesh with the remaining moisture of the pepper. The result is an appearance ranging from deep purple to a dark, purplish black. Urfa biber is less spicy than many other chile peppers but provides a more lasting build-up of heat.

For centuries, these peppers have been used to season kebabs, stews, and sauces. And the fact that the Aleppo pepper has been brought back from near extinction shows the importance of seed banks in preserving the plants and flavors humans come to rely on but too often destroy.

Roasted Ajvar Salsa over Grilled Polenta

INGREDIENTS

1 medium eggplant

2 tbsps. olive oil

5 medium red bell peppers (deveined, deseeded, and sliced in half lengthwise)

8 oz. cooked polenta

2 to 3 tbsps. roasted garlic flakes

1 to 2 tbsps. white wine vinegar

1 tsp. smoked paprika (hot) *or* smoked paprika (sweet)

½ tsp. Aleppo pepper

Aluminum foil

Cooking spray

Plastic wrap

Ajvar can be served as a relish with crusty bread, as a spread combined with other condiments, or prepared and placed on grilled polenta and served as an appetizer or light meal.

INSTRUCTIONS

Preheat grill to high heat. Wash the eggplant and slice it in half longwise. Lightly score the flesh with a paring knife. Brush with a little olive oil to prevent sticking. Lay each ½ pepper on a cutting board (cut side down) and flatten it with the back of your hand. This will help the pepper make better contact with the heat on the grill. Reduce the heat to medium high and place the eggplant flesh-side down on the hot grill. Grill 3 to 4 minutes on each side until the eggplant becomes tender and cooked through. Tear a piece of foil large enough for the polenta and spray lightly with cooking spray. Place the foil on the grill and place polenta on top. Grill about 4 minutes on each side until eggplants are warm and slightly crispy. Remove the eggplant and polenta from the grill to a cutting board to cool. Place the peppers skin-side down on the grill and let them cook until the skins start to blister and blacken. Transfer the peppers to a large bowl and cover the bowl with plastic wrap and allow the peppers to cool. The steam will make the peppers easier to peel. When the eggplant is cool, scoop out the flesh and transfer to food processor. Add the olive oil and garlic and process until smooth. When the peppers are cool, peel off the blistered skin, cut them into strips and add them to the food processor. Add the vinegar, paprika, and Aleppo pepper, pulsing several times to achieve the desired consistency. Serves 4.

INGREDIENTS

Kabobs

3 lbs. boneless beef or lamb cubes

2 tbsps. Turkish seasoning

2 to 3 tsps. Aleppo pepper powder

3 tbsps. olive oil

20 to 24 wooden skewers

Yogurt Dip

1 cup plain low-fat yogurt

2 tsps. Turkish seasoning

½ to 1 tsp. Aleppo pepper powder

¼ cup cucumber (finely chopped)

Turkish Kabobs with Aleppo Pepper

Beef or lamb kabobs marinated with Turkish spices and Aleppo pepper and grilled up crispy brown served with seasoned yogurt make the perfect picnic appetizer. Turkish kabobs also make a great lunch when wrapped in warm pita bread with tomato and onion.

INSTRUCTIONS

Cut the meat into small, ¾ inch cubes. Each piece should be a one-bite morsel. This allows for the crispiest cooking on the grill. Wash the meat and pat dry. Toss with Turkish seasoning, Aleppo pepper, and olive oil. Cover tightly and refrigerate overnight for the best flavor, or at least 2 hours. Soak the skewers in water overnight if possible or for a minimum of 20 minutes—the longer the better. Thread the meat loosely but still touching on the skewers. Keeping the pieces close together near the tip helps prevent burning the skewer. Hibachis were designed for grilling skewers so if you have one this is the time to use it. If not, stack the coals two deep in half the grill. The kabobs should be cooked over high heat, but they can burn the exposed ends of the skewers. If using a full-sized grill, try wrapping the skewer ends with aluminum foil or soaking skewers in water for 20 minutes or up to 3 hours to prevent them from burning. Grill, uncovered, turning every couple of minutes until crispy brown (about 10 minutes). To make the yogurt dip, combine all the ingredients, stirring well, and serve with the kabobs. Serves 10 to 12.

Serrano

The serrano is about five times hotter than the jalapeno. The word *sierra* means mountain in Spanish, so "serrano" is considered a permutation of this word. This pod type originated in the mountains of northern Puebla and Hidalgo, Mexico. The plants are 3 feet high and 1½ feet wide. The leaves are very hairy, giving the plant a silvery appearance. It has cylindrical fruits 2 to 5 inches long and ½ inch wide, with medium-thick walls and no corkiness. The immature fruit color ranges from light to dark green; when mature, the fruits can be any number of colors—red, brown, orange, or yellow. This chile pepper is often chosen for the sharp crisp flavor it gives when incorporated fresh into salsa. Serrano is the chile of choice for making pico de gallo.

In Mexico, serranos are classified into three distinct groups based on the length of the pod. Balin has pods that are 1 to 2 inches long and are conical or elongated in shape and are very firm. This is the "standard" serrano sold in commerce. Tipico has pods that are 2 to 4 inches long, straight, smooth, and have a shape or rounded tip. The Largo pods are more than 4 inches long and are pointed and curved. In the Teaching Garden, there is a special serrano, the NuMex LotaLutein. This serrano has the highest level of lutein of any chile pepper in the world. Lutein has shown to lower the risk for macular degeneration and cataracts. A pico de gallo made with NuMex LotaLutein is both tasty *and* healthy!

(*Opposite page*) Serrano peppers. Image courtesy of Cindy, licensed under CC by 2.0.

4 Roma tomatoes

1 white onion

12 cilantro sprigs

2 serrano chile peppers (deveined, deseeded, and finely chopped)

½ to 1 tsp. sea salt, to taste

1 Mexican lime

Pico de Gallo

This is a raw salsa known in Spanish as a salsa fresca, or fresh salsa. It is delicious with ripe red Roma tomatoes. The flavor is built around the tomatoes and enhanced by the other ingredients. Use it as a topping on beef, chicken, or fish or as a chip dip. You will find it on every Mexican table.

INSTRUCTIONS

Cut the tops off the tomatoes, then slice in half lengthwise. Use a teaspoon to scoop out the seeds and pulp and discard. Remove the cilantro leaves from the stems and discard the stems. Chop the tomato into ¼ inch pieces. Finely chop the onion, cilantro, and serrano chile. Put the chopped ingredients into a mixing bowl. Add the salt and lime juice. Stir until ingredients are mixed evenly. Serve slightly chilled or at room temperature. If you serve it cold, it will taste flat. Pico de gallo is best when eaten fresh.

Sweet Potato Peanut Soup

A satisfying and healthy vegetarian soup everyone will enjoy.

INSTRUCTIONS

Heat the olive oil in a Dutch oven or large pot over medium heat. Add the onion, chile, garlic, and ginger. Sauté until fragrant. Add in the sweet potato followed by the tomato paste, both kinds of coconut milk, water, salt, and turmeric. Simmer for a minimum of 30 minutes or until sweet potatoes are fork tender. Add the peanut butter and peanuts. Stir until well combined. Add the kale and simmer 15 to 45 minutes, until soup reaches desired consistency. Stir in the lime juice and serve with additional peanuts. Serves 8.

INGREDIENTS

2 tbsps. olive oil

1 small onion (diced)

1 serrano (destemmed and minced)

4 garlic cloves (minced)

1½ inch piece ginger root (peeled and minced)

3 large, sweet potatoes (peeled and cubed)

3 tbsps. tomato paste

One 14-oz. can full-fat coconut milk

One 14-oz. can light coconut milk

2 cups water

1 tsp. salt

1 tsp. turmeric

½ cup peanut butter

½ cup peanuts (chopped)

2 cups kale (chopped with stems removed)

1 tbsp. lime juice

Asian Pepper Types

C an one think of Asian food without thinking about the small hot chile peppers used in those dishes? Even though there is a *Capsicum* species, *C. chinense* (which is associated with "China"), no chile peppers are truly native to China or anywhere else in Asia.

Fruit of Takanotsume, translated as "claws of the eagle".

JAPANESE

Japanese chile varieties can be very hot, like the Takanotsume, Hontaka, Yatsufusa, and the Santaka. The hot Asian chiles have fruit that matures from green to red, is upright, measures 2½ inches long and ¼ inches wide, and is set in clusters on the plant. The fruits are considered hot, but the heat dissipates rapidly. Takanotsume translates as "the claw of the eagle," reflecting its talon shape and the fact that it has a heat that is sharp as compared to a flat heat. The sharp heat comes on rapidly, on the tip of the tongue and the front of the mouth, and will dissipate quickly. This is the typical chile pepper found in hot soups at Asian restaurants. Each one of these hot chile pepper varieties is unique and originally grown in specific regions of Japan. Unfortunately, in the Western world, the varieties are often lumped together as "Asian hots" or "Japones," the Spanish word for Japanese.

There are also mild chile peppers originating from Japan, like the Shishito and Fushimi. There are several opinions regarding when chile peppers were introduced to Japan. According to one version, the Portuguese brought them to Japan in 1542 when a Portuguese ship was washed ashore off the coast of Tanegashima at the southern end of Japan. Chile pepper is called *togarashi* in Japan, a word meaning "China." However, while the Japanese falsely assumed the chile pepper had come from China, in fact, it may be that chile peppers were introduced to Japan before they appeared in China.

INGREDIENTS

Lasagna

1 lb. dried lasagna noo-
dles

1 tsp. salt

1 tbsp. olive oil

Filling

1 lb. ricotta cheese

1 egg

3 garlic cloves, minced

1 tbsp. fresh oregano,
chopped

¼ cup fresh basil,
chopped

½ tsp. hot pepper flakes

1 cup parmesan cheese,
grated

1 lb. fresh spinach, large
stems removed

2 to 6 Japanese chile
pepper pods (roasted,
peeled, destemmed,
deseeded, and chopped)

(continued on next page)

Pepper Garden "Surprise" Lasagna

We're calling this lasagna recipe "Surprise" because you may decide to include in your recipe anything from the mild Shishito to the fiery Takanotsume. This one is your call. Roasting, chopping, or even using a powdered version of your chosen pepper will give you flexibility in heat and flavor.

INSTRUCTIONS

Boil a large pot of water. Add the lasagna noodles and salt to the water and cook for 9 minutes or just until the noodles are tender. Drain the noodles and sepa-rate them. Brush each lasagna noodle lightly with olive oil so they do not stick together. Set aside. In a small bowl, blend the ricotta with the egg, garlic, oregano, basil, pepper flakes, and 2 tbsps. parmesan cheese. Set aside. Wash the spinach. Steam the spinach until just wilted, about 1 minute. Squeeze out some of the liquid and set the spinach aside. To make the bécha-mel sauce, melt the butter in a heavy saucepan. Using a wire whisk, stir in the flour. Add the milk, a little at a time, while stirring. Simmer over low to medium heat until the sauce thickens, stirring constantly to avoid lumps and burning the bottom of the pan. Once the sauce thickens, cook it for 1 minute longer. Season the sauce with nutmeg, salt, and pepper. To assemble the lasagna, preheat the oven to 350°F. Brush the bottom of a large 14-inch x 9-inch x 2-inch baking dish with olive oil. Cover the bottom of the dish with a single layer of lasagna noodles. Spread the ricotta mixture over the noodles. Cover the ricotta with your choice of 2 to 6 Japanese peppers and sprinkle with ½ cup mozzarella. Cover with a layer of noodles. Spread the spinach over the noodles and cover with the béchamel sauce and another ½ cup of mozzarella. Cover with a last layer of noodles and sprinkle them with another ½ cup of mozzarella. Pour the marinara sauce over the lasagna. Sprinkle it with the remaining mozzarella and parmesan cheese. Bake the lasagna for 30 to 40 minutes or until the cheese is lightly browned and bubbly. Let the lasagna sit for about 10 minutes after removing it from the oven so the juices will be absorbed before serving. Serves 6 to 8.

2 cups mozzarella cheese, grated

3½ cups marinara sauce

Béchamel Sauce

2 tbsps. butter

3 tbsps. flour

2 cups milk

Pinch of nutmeg

Salt and pepper to taste

Scallops with Takanotsume Peppers

Have you tried sea scallops? They are a larger scallop variety with a chewy meat and a sweet flavor. The have a pleasant sea food taste without being fishy. Shellfish take on the seasoning that you cook them with, so be prepared for a tasty dish.

INSTRUCTIONS

Heat a large sauté pan over medium-high heat. When the pan is hot, add the oil and sear the scallops for 15 to 30 seconds on each side. Remove from the pan and set aside. Add the garlic and the Takanotsume pepper into the pan. Gently agitate the pan to cook the ingredients until the oil becomes aromatic. Carefully deglaze with sake while the pan is off the heat. Return the pan to the heat. Add the soy sauce, mirin, brown sugar, rice vinegar, ginger, and corn starch solution. Bring to a boil, lower to a simmer, and cook until thickened. Add the scallops back to the pan and toss to coat and heat through. Serves 5.

INGREDIENTS

1 tbsp. peanut oil

1 lb. sea scallops

1 tbsp. garlic

3 to 4 Takanotsume peppers (deseeded and julienned)

¼ cup sake

½ cup soy sauce

½ cup mirin (rice wine)

3 tbsps. brown sugar

¼ cup rice vinegar

1½ tbsps. ginger (grated)

1 tbsp. corn starch *or* potato starch (dissolved in cold water)

KOREAN

Korea has its own chile peppers. *Gochu*, meaning "pepper" in Korean, is a popular chile. The red color and hot taste of hot pepper powder is used as a key ingredient for the well-known Korean delicacies kimchi and gochujang. Kimchi is a pickled Chinese cabbage or Japanese radish mixed with hot pepper powder, chopped garlic, and other seasonings before fermentation. Gochujang is a fermented paste of dried pepper powder mixed well with other ingredients, such as fermented soybean powder, wheat flour, and boiled rice or barley. Both can be preserved for long periods.

INGREDIENTS

8 oz. uncooked whole wheat thin spaghetti *or* linguine (cook as directed)

¼ cup scallions (chopped, including both green and white parts)

½ cup shredded carrots

1 tbsp. canola oil

2 tbsps. sesame oil

1 tbsp. Asian chile pepper flakes

3 tbsps. honey

3 tbsps. low sodium soy sauce

2 tbsps. dried cilantro

1 tsp. toasted sesame seeds

1 tsp. black sesame seeds

Spicy Thai Noodles

See if you notice the spicy yet sweet hint of flavors this dish offers. Made from common ingredients, it might just become a go-to last minute favorite meal or side dish.

INSTRUCTIONS

Drain the noodles and add them to a medium bowl. Add scallions and carrots to the noodles and toss. In a small pan, heat both oils together to medium heat. Add the Asian chile powder and sauté for about 30 seconds. Strain out the pepper flakes and reserve the infused oil. Let cool. In a small bowl, whisk together the oil, honey, and soy sauce. Add the oil mixture, cilantro, and sesame seeds to the noodles and toss. Serve immediately or chill overnight and serve cold. Serves 4.

Korean Kimchi

Kimchi is a salted and fermented cabbage dish and is a staple eaten at every Korean meal. When traveling to South Korea you will see every piece of land (even some road medians) planted with cabbage to provide Koreans with their daily supply of kimchi.

INSTRUCTIONS

Place the cabbage in a large bowl and sprinkle with salt. Place a heavy pot or pan on top with weights and allow the cabbage to sit for 1 to 2 hours until it is wilted and water has been released. Discard the water. Rinse the cabbage 2 to 3 times in the sink until the salt is removed and allow to drain in a colander for another 15 to 20 minutes. Combine the cabbage with the remaining ingredients except the Korean red pepper flakes, and mix. Using gloves, add the pepper flakes and begin mixing and rubbing them into the mixture. Once combined, place mixture in a jar, pressing down and packing tightly so that the mixture is submerged in its own liquid. Place the top on the jar and place the jar on a plate (the mixture may bubble over) and allow to sit at room temperature for 2 to 5 days. Serve at room temperature or heated. Serves 6 to 8.

INGREDIENTS

1 cabbage (cut into 2-inch strips)

¼ to ½ cup kosher salt

2 tbsps. garlic cloves (minced)

2 tbsps. ginger (minced)

1 tsp. sugar

1 large daikon radish (peeled and cut into 1-inch matchsticks)

2 bunches green onions (cut into 1-inch pieces)

3 tbsps. water

4 tbsps. Korean red pepper flakes

Piment d'Espelette

The whitewashed Basque town of Espelette is famous for its dark red chile pepper, an integral ingredient in traditional Basque cuisine. The Espelette pepper or Piment d'Espelette ("pepper from Espelette," in French) came to the United States from France. The unique aspect of this chile pepper is that it has "appellation" designation. An appellation is usually associated with wines and is a designated growing area governed by the rules and regulations established by the federal government and the local governing body. The French initiated the Appellation d'origine contrôlêe (AOC) system in 1935 to safeguard their quality winemakers, vineyards, and regions from unethical producers who could otherwise take advantage of better-known wine names.

In 1999 the French National Institute for Trade Name Origins issued an AOC for the Espelette chile pepper and its products. Thus, the Espelette chile pepper name is protected just like that of Champagne and Roquefort cheese. Espelette chile peppers can only be grown in southern France in the region sometimes known as Basque Country, in the towns of Espelette, Ainhoa, Cambo-les-Bains, Halsou, Itxassou, Jatxou, Laressore, Saint-Pée-sur-Nivelle, Souraide, and Ustaritz. In this area, the arrival of autumn means the facades of houses will become embellished by their famous bright red chile pepper ristras, reminiscent of what is found in the US Southwest. The chile peppers dry out in the sun before being reduced to a rich, burgundy-colored powder that is used to adorn the very best of Basque foods. This proud tradition dates to the sixteenth century in France; by the eighteenth century, the region was famous for its chile peppers. Since then, the success of the Espelette chile pepper has achieved legendary status and every first Sunday of October a large festival is held in the chile pepper's honor. The Espelette chile pepper is a mildly hot short red chile pepper that goes well with chicken, lamb, and fish. As with wine, we can't guarantee that the Espelette pepper you grow in your garden will have the flavor and aroma of the Espelette chile pepper grown in France, but it won't hurt to try!

Chicken Basquaise with Piperade

This delicious dish goes well with boiled potatoes and green beans.

½ cup olive oil

4 medium onions (chopped)

3 garlic cloves

4 green bell peppers (destemmed, deseeded, and chopped)

2 red bell peppers (destemmed, deseeded, and chopped)

4 large tomatoes (peeled and chopped)

3 tbsps. ground Piment d'Espelette, or more to taste

1 pinch thyme

1 chicken (cut up)

Salt and pepper

INSTRUCTIONS

Heat ¼ cup olive oil in a large frying pan and sauté the onions and garlic for 5 minutes, stirring occasionally. Add the bell peppers and cook over medium heat for 10 minutes. Add the tomatoes and Espelette powder and cook for 20 minutes, stirring occasionally. Add the thyme, salt, and pepper and transfer to a bowl. Wipe out the pan and heat the remaining ¼ cup of oil. Brown the chicken in the oil until golden, turning often. Pour the Piperade over the chicken, reduce the heat, cover and simmer until tender, about 30 to 40 minutes. Add salt and pepper to taste. Serves 6.

INGREDIENTS

1½ tbsps. shallots (finely chopped)

2 tsps. fresh lemon juice

2 tsps. sherry wine vinegar

1½ tsps. lime peel (finely chopped)

1 cup mayonnaise

1 tsp. Piment d'Espelette powder or finely chopped pepper

Coarse sea salt

Black pepper (freshly ground)

Piment d'Espelette Mayonnaise

If you are a fan of mayonnaise, you'll find many uses for this recipe. We like it as a sandwich condiment.

INSTRUCTIONS

Combine the shallots, lemon juice, vinegar, and lime peel in a medium bowl. Cover and let stand 30 minutes. Whisk in mayonnaise and Piment d'Espelette. Season with salt and pepper. Cover and chill 2 hours. Can be made 1 day ahead. Keep chilled. Yields 1 cup.

Mirasol, Guajillo, and Cascabel

These three chile peppers are sometimes called the mirasol family. Their fruits share characteristics like subtle flavors and low-to-medium heat levels. Most recipes state that they can be used interchangeably, but there are flavor and heat profile differences. Often these pods are ground into powder in the home and used to make sauces or to add a mild heat and fruity flavor to stews and soups.

MIRASOL

The Spanish word *mirasol* means pointing to the sun and reflects the way the pods are held erect on the plant. In the Teaching Garden, one finds the cultivar NuMex Mirasol, which was released in 1993 by the NMSU breeding program because New Mexico chile producers requested a mirasol chile adapted to New Mexico. NuMex Mirasol has a fasciculate fruit habit, meaning these peppers have branches that end in a fruit cluster, making them perfect for use as an ornamental on wreaths and for being dried and ground into a cooking powder. NuMex Mirasol produces abundant crops of 3-to-5-inches-long, thin-skinned red peppers, conical in shape and medium hot, about 5,000 Scoville Heat Units. The fruits have a unique flavor that is fruity and berrylike and can be described as full-bodied, distinct, and "delicate."

(Opposite page)
NuMex Mirasol.

Gourmet Sliced Pork with Mirasol Peppers

Serve with potato pancakes or applesauce.

INSTRUCTIONS

Clean the pork of excess fat and slice into thin, small strips. Season with salt and pepper and mix with the egg yolks. Let sit for 30 minutes. Add the onion, curry, and sliced chiles. If you are using fresh peppers, 1 to 2 is enough (depending on the size). You can decrease the heat by deveining and deseeding the peppers. Pickled peppers have a different, milder taste. Add the cornstarch to the meat and carefully mix. Heat the oil in heavy duty pan and add the meat mixture. Stir and mix with a wooden spoon on medium-high heat until brown on all sides. Baste with a little bit of the juice from pickled chiles. Wine is fine too if you are using fresh peppers. Serves 4 to 6.

INGREDIENTS

1 lb. pork

Salt and pepper

2 egg yolks

1 small onion (finely chopped)

1 tbsp. curry powder

3 pickled NuMex Mirasol peppers (sliced) *or* a mix of pickled chiles, fresh cayennes, or jalapenos

2 tbsp. cornstarch

2 tbsps. oil

Baked Pumpkin Side Dish

INGREDIENTS

3 lbs. pumpkin
(deseeded and sliced
into 6 wedges)

Vegetable oil

Salt to taste

6 tbsps. butter

¼ cup brown sugar

½ tsp. cinnamon (ground)

¼ tsp. NuMex Mirasol
powder

¼ tsp. coriander (ground)

Sweetly spiced and everything with this dish is truly nice.

INSTRUCTIONS

Preheat oven to 350°F. Place the pumpkin wedges in a shallow baking dish. Coat the wedges thinly with the vegetable oil, sprinkle with salt, and bake for 50 to 55 minutes or until soft. In a small pan, melt the butter and mix it with the remaining ingredients. Keep the mixture warm. Spoon the butter mixture over the pumpkin wedges. Bake for an additional 10 to 15 minutes until the pumpkin can be punctured easily with a fork. Serves 6.

GUAJILLO

The guajillo, sometimes referred to as "pulla" or "puya," has a beautiful translucent skin and a subtle flavor with slightly fruity undertones. These are among the most common dried chile peppers used in Mexican cuisine but are not common in the United States. As with other dried chile peppers, buy ones that are still pliable. They can still be used if they are brittle, but some of their flavor will have faded by the time they get to that point. Typically, the guajillo is sold as a whole dried pod and is a bit more difficult to find in the powder or ground form. Because they have a mild heat (2,500 to 5,000 SHUs), they are frequently blended with other dried chile peppers to supply the heat. For example, guajillo is often paired with chile de arbols and anchos. The pods change from green to a rich burgundy. They are native to central and northern Mexico and are one of the most widely grown chile peppers in Aguascalientes, Durango, San Luis Potosi, and Zacatecas, Mexico. Guajillo is often substituted for mulato chile pepper and combined with ancho and pasilla pods to make Mexican moles.

Spicy Pomodoro Pasta Sauce

This is a versatile sauce and is simple to make. Be sure to use Parmigiano Reggiano cheese and lots of garlic. Serve it over your favorite pasta. Make it into a complete meal by adding chicken or shrimp. This sauce also works as a dipping sauce for chicken fingers or your other favorite dipping food.

INGREDIENTS

2 tsps. olive oil

6 garlic cloves (chopped)

4 medium–sized tomatoes

2 tsps. salt

1 tsp. black pepper

1 tsp. guajillo pepper (crushed)

2 tbsps. balsamic vinegar

15 basil leaves (chopped)

⅓ cup Parmigiano Reggiano

INSTRUCTIONS

Heat the oil over medium heat in a small sauté pan. Add the garlic, sauté until fragrant (about 1 minute). Add the tomatoes, salt, pepper, and red pepper flakes and stir. Continue to sauté tomatoes until they begin to fall apart. Add the balsamic vinegar and heat for 5 to 8 more minutes until flavors are combined and the tomatoes have become a chunky sauce. Take the sauce off the heat and stir in the basil and Parmigiano Reggiano. Serves 4.

Mexican-Style Rotisserie Chicken

There are so many recipes for a rotisserie chicken, but this one ranks as one of the best!

INSTRUCTIONS

Grind small quantities of the guajillo and de arbor chiles with oregano in a coffee grinder until the ingredients are well combined and finely ground. Use your washed or gloved hands to spread the garlic salt inside the chicken. Combine the lime juice, minced garlic, and finely ground chile and oregano powder. Use a basting brush to pat most of the mixture over the entire outer surface of the chicken. Set the brush and remaining mixture aside. Place the chicken on a spit in a rotisserie over medium heat for 30 minutes. Recoat the chicken with any remaining chile spice mixture using the basting brush. Grill for another 30 minutes or until the internal temperature of the chicken's thigh measures 165°F. Remove from the spit and allow to cool for about 10 minutes. Carve the chicken for serving. Serve over rice or with a side of beans, warmed tortillas, and a side of salsa. Serves 4 to 6.

INGREDIENTS

1 guajillo chile (deveined and deseeded)

3 chiles de arbol (deveined and deseeded)

1 tsp. dried oregano

3 tsp. garlic salt

3 to 4 lbs. whole chicken (washed and towel dried)

Juice of 2 limes

4 garlic cloves (minced)

12 corn tortillas

CASCABEL

Cascabel means "rattle" in Spanish. This pepper's spherical pod rattles when dried because of the loose seeds inside. The cascabel, also known as "chile bola," has a dark, brown-colored skin and a spherical shape ranging in size from 1 to 1½ inches in diameter. It is unique because of its taste and aroma. The chile peppers are rather mild (1,300 to 2,000 SHUs) and sweet. The flavor is incomparable: rustic, nutty, and smoky, with a tobacco note. This chile pepper is excellent in sauces, soups, and other cooked dishes.

INGREDIENTS

1 tbsp. vegetable oil

1 large onion (chopped)

2 garlic cloves (minced)

Cooking spray

Twelve 6-inch corn tortillas (cut into 1-inch pieces)

2 cups low-fat Monterey Jack cheese (shredded)

4 pickled, fresh, or dried cascabel chile peppers (deveined, deseeded, and chopped)

4 eggs (lightly beaten)

2 cups low-fat buttermilk

½ tsp. salt

½ tsp. ground black pepper

½ to ¾ tsp. ground cumin

¾ tsp. dried oregano (crushed)

¾ tsp. onion powder

Salsa (optional)

Chilaquiles

Chilaquiles are considered a Mexican "comfort" food, eaten for breakfast or lunch. Many regional variations on the dish exist but its continued popularity stems from its short preparation time, inexpensive ingredients, and easy-to-prepare steps.

INSTRUCTIONS

Preheat oven to 375°F. In a large skillet heat the oil over medium heat. Add the onion and garlic and cook until tender. Meanwhile, coat a 2-quart rectangular baking dish with cooking spray. Spread half of the tortilla pieces in the bottom of the prepared baking dish. Top with half of the cheese and 2 of the cascabel chile peppers. Sprinkle with the onion and garlic mixture. Top with the remaining tortilla pieces, cheese, and chile peppers. In a large bowl combine the eggs, buttermilk, salt, black pepper, cumin, and oregano. Pour evenly over the ingredients in the baking dish. Bake for 35 to 40 minutes or until the center is set and the edges are lightly browned. Let stand 15 minutes before serving. Serve with salsa, if desired. Serves 8.

Cascabel Caramel Turtles

These turtles are like no others you've ever tasted—both hot and sweet.

INSTRUCTIONS

In a microwave mixing bowl, combine the caramels and whipped topping. Cook on 50 percent power for 45 seconds. Remove the bowl, stir, and place back in the microwave. Continue this process in 10-second increments until the mixture has completely melted and is smooth and well-blended. Let the mixture cool slightly. Spray a cookie sheet lightly with the cooking spray. Place the pecan halves on the sheet in groups of five, arranged so that each group forms a shape like a turtle's body with four legs. Carefully spoon the caramel mixture over each, leaving the ends of the pecans showing. Set aside until the caramel has hardened. Place the chocolate chips in a microwave bowl. Cook in the microwave on 50 percent power for 45 seconds, remove, stir, and repeat the process in 10-second intervals until the chocolate is melted and smooth. Stir in the cascabels and let the chocolate mixture cool slightly. Spoon the melted chocolate over the caramel, being careful not to cover the exposed ends of the pecans. Set aside until hard, then store in a covered container in a cool place. Yield: 15.

INGREDIENTS

24 soft caramels

2 tbsps. whipped topping

Butter–flavored vegetable cooking spray

75 pecan halves

4 oz. semisweet chocolate chips

8 cascabel chile peppers (dried, destemmed, deveined, deseeded, and finely chopped)

U p until this point in the Teaching Garden all the chile peppers we've encountered belong to the same species, *C. annuum*. Now we venture into some of the other species. Of the five domesticated chile pepper species, *C. frutescens* has the fewest pod shapes, sizes, and colors. The first cultivar is well-known, made famous by the renowned sauce maker Mr. McIlhenny: Tabasco. In addition to Tabasco, *C. frutescens* includes the malagueta pepper, the Thai, and the Siling Labuyo. The hot sauce produced by this species provides a unique flavor profile and heat sensation.

Tabasco

T abasco is probably one of the best-known chile pepper varieties in the world because of its hot sauce affiliation. Tabasco is a state in Mexico, where it is believed the pod originated. Tabasco pepper sauce measures 2,500–5,000 Scoville heat units and is a major ingredient in creole cooking. Today, Tabasco-brand pepper sauce is sold in more than 185 countries and territories and is packaged in 22 languages and dialects. Whole pods can be placed in jars to make spicy vinegar. The yellow, orange, or red fruits make a nice ornamental addition to the garden.

(*Opposite page*)
Tabasco plant
growing in the
Teaching Garden.

Cajun-Style Hot Wings

INGREDIENTS

½ lb. chicken wings (12 to 15 wings)

Oil to deep fry wings

¼ cup Tabasco sauce

1 tsp. onion powder

1 tsp. garlic powder

½ tsp. dried thyme

½ tsp. dried oregano

½ cup butter or margarine (melted)

This wing recipe is delicious and can be made as spicy or as mild as you like. Try it with your favorite Mexican beer.

INSTRUCTIONS

Split the wings at each joint and discard the tips. Pat dry. Deep fry at 400°F for 12 minutes or until completely cooked and crispy. Drain. While the wings are cooking, combine the Tabasco sauce, onion powder, garlic powder, thyme, and oregano with the melted butter and simmer for 2 minutes to blend the flavors. Dip the fried wings into the sauce and coat completely. Serve with your favorite dip. Yields 24 to 30 pieces.

Nonalcoholic Bloody Mary

Make a jug of spiky Bloody Mary mix for a weekend brunch that won't make you feel fuzzy.

INSTRUCTIONS

Put everything in a big jug and mix. Add a handful of crushed ice, if desired. Serves 1 to 2.

INGREDIENTS

1¾ pints tomato juice

1 bunch celery leaves (washed and picked from celery bunch)

Dash Tabasco sauce, to taste

Dash creamed horse-radish

Dash brown sauce, to taste

2 limes (juice only)

Crushed ice (optional)

Malagueta

The name "malagueta" is derived from a plant from Africa called *malegueta* in Portuguese and Grains-of-Paradise in English. This relative of ginger has no botanical relationship to chile peppers, and the similarity of names has caused more than one source to suggest an African origin for Brazilian malagueta peppers. This is not true: malagueta peppers originated in the New World. Small malagueta peppers grow no larger than about 2 inches and turn from green to red when ripened. The malagueta has a heat level anywhere from 60,000 to 100,000 SHUs. Although the malagueta is cultivated and consumed throughout Brazil, it is most strongly associated with the cooking and food traditions of the state of Bahia (Brazil's fourth largest state). It is used to liven soups and stews and a bottle of malagueta hot sauce is found on every Bahian table.

Saltine-Crusted Fish with Malagueta Honey Butter

INGREDIENTS

28 saltine crackers

½ cup flour

4 eggs, beaten

1 shallot, diced

½ cup dry white wine

½ cup champagne vinegar

3 sprigs fresh thyme

¼ cup heavy cream

2 sticks unsalted butter, cut into cubes

2 tsps. malagueta pepper powder *or* red powder flakes, if malagueta is hard to find

5 tbsps. honey

Salt and pepper

2 oz. extra virgin olive oil

two 6-oz. pieces of fresh white fish

Pick your favorite white fish and you will experience a whole new way to enjoy it with this recipe!

INSTRUCTIONS

Preheat oven to 350°F. Use a food processor to crush the saltine crackers into very fine crumbs. Place the crumbs on a plate. Place the flour on a second plate and the eggs in a shallow bowl in between the two plates. Make the butter sauce by combing the shallots, wine, vinegar, and fresh thyme in a medium pot. Bring to a rapid boil and cook until the mixture has reduced by two thirds. Add the heavy cream and reduce again by two thirds or until the mixture becomes thick. Once the mixture is reduced, slowly whisk in the butter while stirring rapidly. After the butter is completely mixed in, strain the sauce to remove the thyme and shallot pieces. Stir in the malagueta powder and honey and season with salt and pepper. Heat the olive oil in a large oven-proof sauté pan. Season the fish on both the top and underside with salt and pepper. Dredge the fish in the flour, shaking off any excess. Dip the fish in the egg and then coat with saltine crumbs. Place the fish in the pan and sear on both sides until golden brown. Transfer to the oven and cook for about 10 minutes or until thoroughly cooked. Serve hot with the sauce spooned on top. Serves 2.

Grilled Spring Asparagus

No, you can't use canned or frozen asparagus! This recipe only works with fresh asparagus, so take advantage of the months when you can either gather the asparagus from your garden or buy it fresh at your local farmer's market. Your taste buds will thank you. Consider this recipe as an accompaniment to grilled fish.

INSTRUCTIONS

Combine the olive oil, lemon juice, chile, garlic, parsley, and black pepper. Mix well. Cut off the tough asparagus stems, rinse, and place in a shallow bowl. Pour the spice mix over the asparagus and allow to marinate at room temperature for at least an hour. Grill the asparagus over medium heat for 2 minutes on each side or until done but still crisp. Serve immediately or keep in a covered dish until served. Serves 4.

INGREDIENTS

3 tbsps. olive oil

2 tbsps. lemon juice, freshly squeezed

2 malagueta chile pods (destemmed, deseeded, and finely chopped)

2 garlic cloves, minced

2 tsps. parsley *or* rosemary, fresh and finely chopped

Black pepper

1 lb. asparagus, fresh

Thai

Thai chile peppers are a mixed bag of types. They can be *C. annuum*, *C. chinense*, and *C. frutescens*. While many different varieties of chile peppers are found in Thai cuisine, the most common one is the *prik kee noo*, which is a *C. frutescens*. Professor Suchila Techawongstien at Kon Kaen University in Thailand has stated that there are at least eighty different types of chile peppers within the three species grown in Thailand. Thus confusion regarding what, specifically, is a Thai chile pepper is understandable. In Thailand, the chile peppers are called *prik*, with descriptive adjectives added. For example, one finds *prik chee fah*, meaning "chile pepper pointing to the sky," which is the most popular chile used in Thai cuisine. The *prik kee noo* (prik ki nu) translates to "mouse dropping chile pepper"—because of its tiny size—and is known to be one of the hottest found in Thailand. This is the Thai chile pepper most commonly sold in North America. Sriracha, a name associated with another famous sauce originally made from Thai chile peppers in the Thai seaside town of the same name, is made with red jalapenos in the United States!

Thai Bird Pepper Sauces

*We love playing around with these simple chile pepper sauces—
drizzle them on Pad Thai, fried rice, omelets, just about anything for
some heat. These peppers are very hot, so just use the sauce (don't eat
the chile pepper pods) if you want the flavor but not the heat.*

INSTRUCTIONS

Place the chile peppers in a small bowl. Add the vinegar and fish sauce or kecap manis. Wisk the ingredients together. Keep in the refrigerator between uses.

Chile Pepper Vinegar Sauce

1 tbsp. Thai chile pepper (minced)

¼ cup coconut or white vinegar

Chile Pepper Fish Sauce

1 tbsp. Thai chile pepper (minced)

¼ cup fish sauce (your favorite brand)

Chile Pepper Sweet Soy Sauce

1 tbsp. Thai chile pepper (minced)

¼ cup kecap manis (sweet soy sauce)

INGREDIENTS

1 tbsp. corn oil *or* sunflower oil

1 garlic glove (crushed)

2 lemongrass stalks (outer leaves removed and finely chopped)

1-inch piece of ginger root (peeled and grated)

2 to 3 Thai red peppers (deveined, deseeded and chopped)

1½ cup chicken breast (shredded skinless, and boneless)

1 tbsp. soy sauce

2 tsp. Thai fish sauce

1 cup bean sprouts

1 small iceberg lettuce head (separated into leaves)

Dipping Sauce

2 tbsps. Thai fish sauce

2 garlic cloves (minced)

1 to 2 tbsps. sugar

2 tbsps. lime juice

2 tbsps. white wine vinegar

1 Thai chile pepper pod (deveined, deseeded, and finely chopped)

Thai Picnic Packages

These delicious hand salad treats will be a hit at your next picnic.

INSTRUCTIONS

Mix all the sauce ingredients together in a small bowl, cover, and set aside for at least 30 minutes. Heat the oil in a large saucepan and stir-fry the garlic, lemongrass, ginger, and chile pods for 2 minutes. Add the chicken and continue to stir-fry for 5 minutes or until the chicken is cooked. Add the soy sauce and fish sauce, stirring once. Then add the bean sprouts and stir-fry for another 30 seconds. Arrange a heaping spoonful of the chicken mixture on each lettuce leaf and drizzle with a little sauce. Roll up to form a square package. Serve the treats on a platter and place the remaining sauce in a bowl for dipping. Serves 6.

Siling Labuyo

In the Philippines, the most notable chile pepper is the Siling Labuyo, which can be broken down as *siling* (chile pepper) and *labuyo* (wild): thus, it is a feral chile pepper. The progenitor of the Siling Labuyo is said to have made its way to the Philippines via Mexico on a galleon trade ship that traveled between Acapulco and Manila. After years of growing wild and adapting to the soil and climate of the Philippines, the Siling Labuyo was born, a landrace for the Philippines. According to folklore, it spread by wild chickens that feasted on the fruits. In the past, one could find Siling Labuyo growing in most Filipino backyard gardens but today they are more difficult to find. The Siling Labuyo chile pepper was added to the Slow Food Arc of Taste in 2014, a database of food items that are at risk of extinction. Slow Food aims to educate the public to preserve these foods for future generations.

Siling Labuyo flavor pairs well with shellfish, seafood, chicken, sautéed vegetables, papaya, mango, sweet potato, ginger, garlic, onion, sugarcane, vinegar, soy sauce, and coconut milk. The Luzon Islands of Mindanao and Bicol in the central Philippines are renowned for their spicy cuisine, which prominently features this pepper. The pepper pods are commonly used in a dish known as *gulay na lada* or bicol express, which consists of Siling Labuyo chile peppers and coconut milk. The leaves, known as *dahon ng sili*, are also utilized and are a popular ingredient in Filipino dishes such as monggo and chicken tinola. The Siling Labuyo is an indispensable ingredient in some of the cuisines of the Maranao, Visayan, and Bicolano tribes. In the Visayas and Mindanao regions, a raw fish dish called *kinilaw* is not complete without Siling Labuyo. Siling Labuyo is also used to spice up canned or bottled sardines and commercially sold vinegar. It is also added in a condiment or dip for broiled pork or fish and roasted meat for a spicy hot meal.

Tinolang Manok
(Chicken with Papaya Soup)

A Filipino favorite.

INSTRUCTIONS

Sprinkle the chicken pieces with salt. Set aside. In a stockpot, sauté the ginger and onions over medium high heat for 2 minutes. Add the chicken and cook for 4 minutes or until the meat is no longer pink. Add the fish sauce and stir to combine flavor. Add the water, let boil, lower heat, and simmer for 30 minutes or until the meat is cooked. Add the papaya and cook for 5 minutes or until the papaya pieces are tender. Correct seasonings by adding fish sauce or salt. Add the spinach or Siling Labuyo leaves and two pieces of pepper. Cover and remove from the heat. Let stand for 5 minutes before serving. Serves 4 to 6.

INGREDIENTS

2 lbs. skinless chicken (thighs or chicken pieces of your choice)

1 thumb–sized ginger (peeled and julienned)

1 medium onion (chopped)

2 tbsps. olive oil

1 tbsp. fish sauce *or* salt

12 cups water

1 semi–ripe papaya (peeled, deseeded, and cut into cubes)

Small bunch spinach leaves *or* Siling Labuyo leaves

2 pieces Siling Labuyo chile peppers (2 pieces, ½ inch x ½ inch each)

Kinilaw na tuna (Raw Tuna Salad)

This "raw" fish salad is made from fresh tuna mixed with vinegar, garlic, onion, ginger, lime juice, salt, and pepper. It is quite similar to ceviche. The fish becomes partially cooked by the time it is served due to the interaction with the vinegar and calamansi juice (a Filipino version of lemonade and limeade). It's served as a pulutan—an accompaniment to an alcoholic drink.

INSTRUCTIONS

Place the cubed tuna meat in a large bowl then pour in ¾ cups of vinegar. Let stand for 2 minutes, then gently squeeze the tuna by placing a spoon on top and applying a little pressure. Gently wash the tuna meat with vinegar. Drain all the vinegar once done. This will help reduce the fishy smell. Add the remaining ¾ cup vinegar, calamansi or lemon juice, ginger, salt, ground black pepper, and Siling Labuyo chile pepper and mix well. Cover the bowl and refrigerate for at least 2 hours. Top with minced red onions and serve. Serves 8.

INGREDIENTS

2 lbs. fresh tuna (skinned, deboned, and cubed)

1½ cups vinegar

½ cup lemon *or* calamansi juice

3 tbsps. ginger (minced)

2 tsps. salt

1 tsp. black pepper (ground)

1 to 2 tbsps. Siling Labuyo pod (chopped)

1 large red onion (minced)

NuMex NoBasco

The name of the cultivar NuMex NoBasco is a paronomasia (pun) because Tabasco is hot with a heat level of approximately 30,000 Scoville Heat Units, while NuMex NoBasco has no heat, i.e., zero Scoville Heat Units. NuMex NoBasco has a similar fruit color, shape, and size to Tabasco. Low or no-heat chile peppers are indispensable to commercial salsa and hot sauce makers have used them for years to reduce the heat in mass-produced salsas and hot sauces. Taking away the heat does not affect the flavor essence of a chile pepper, which retains all the fruity and floral notes. NuMex NoBasco originated from a hybridization between Tabasco and a no-heat *C. frutescens* accession from Colombia.

INGREDIENTS

Seed Bowl

3 tbsps. pumpkin seeds

3 tbsps. sunflower seeds

3 tbsps. pine nuts

3 tbsps. sesame seeds *or* chia seeds

1 tbsp. honey

2 to 3 NoBasco chile peppers (deseeded and finely chopped)

¼ tsp. paprika

Pinch of sea salt

Brunch Bowl

4 large handfuls of watercress

2 ripe avocados (destoned and cut into small chunks)

20 cherry tomatoes (quartered)

4 scallions (finely sliced)

1 handful of fresh cilantro (finely chopped)

4 tbsps. olive oil

Lemon juice

Salt and pepper, to taste

8 eggs (beaten)

3 tbsps. butter

Avocado and Scrambled Egg Brunch Bowl

Be cautious with this recipe because your family will be asking for it every weekend!

INSTRUCTIONS

Place a large frying pan on medium heat and add the pumpkin seeds, sunflower seeds, and pine nuts in the pan. Toast gently for 5 minutes, stirring frequently and turning them until they are golden brown. Add the sesame seeds and continue toasting for another 2 minutes, stirring constantly. Add the honey and chopped peppers and stir for another 2 minutes. Add the sea salt and paprika, stirring for 2 more minutes until the bottom of the frying pan looks dry again and the moisture from the honey has evaporated. Pour the seed mixture onto parchment paper, spreading it out evenly. Allow to cool.

Chop, quarter, and slice the vegetables and herbs and place in a mixing bowl. Pour 2 tbsps. of olive oil and ½ the lemon juice over the ingredients and add a small amount of salt and pepper. Toss gently until ingredients are fully mixed. Set aside. Divide the watercress into 4 shallow bowls and add a little avocado and tomato salad to each. Whisk the eggs in a separate mixing bowl, seasoning with salt and pepper. Place a large nonstick frying pan on medium heat and add the butter. Just as the butter starts to melt, add the whisked eggs. Stir gently until cooked to your liking. Once cooked, divide the eggs between the 4 bowls. Drizzle eggs with the remaining 2 tbsps. olive oil and lemon juice. Then top with the remaining seed mixture. Serves 4.

Breakfast Bacon

Surprise your house guests with this subtle but enhanced flavor to their morning bacon.

INSTRUCTIONS

Remove the bacon from its package and spread each slice out in a large frying pan. Adjust stove heat and when the bacon is ready to turn over (about halfway through the frying process), drain about half of the bacon grease, saving ¼ cup and placing it into a smaller frying pan. Place a smaller pan on medium heat. Add the brown sugar and the chopped chile, stirring until the mixture is thoroughly heated and sugar is melted. Baste the grease, sugar, and chile mixture evenly over the turned bacon. Continue frying the bacon until it's fully cooked. Gently remove bacon strips and drain on paper towels. Serve immediately. Serves 6 to 8.

INGREDIENTS

1 pack of your favorite bacon

¼ cup brown sugar

2 to 3 NuMex NoBasco chile pods (deseeded and finely chopped)

Capsicum baccatum

N ow in our travels in the Teaching Garden we head to South America, where a chile pepper is commonly called *aji* (pronounced "a-hee"). This species is easy to identify because the key is the characteristic yellow or tan spots on the petals of the flowers—an easy trait to view in the Teaching Garden when the plants are blooming. In Peru, the aji is the most popular ingredient in regional dishes and is sometimes known as the "Peruvian chile pepper." Aji was a word brought by the Spanish to Peru from the native Arawak peoples of the Caribbean. In the Quechuan language of the Peruvian Incas, chile peppers are called *uchu*.

The ajis are popular not only as a hot spice but for the subtle bouquet of distinct flavors. They contain a wonderful array of colors, pod shapes, and flavors with strong fruity overtones and berry notes. They are among the most aromatic of all chile peppers.

Our Teaching Garden favorites are the Aji Amarillo, also called Aji Escabeche with bright orange mature fruit, and the Aji Limon, a bright yellow maturing to bright red. An unusual pod is the Bishop's Crown (aka Orchid/Christmas bell) variety, which has a unique fruit shape. The Omnicolor, Aji Limon and Aji Panca are exceptions because they are *Capsicum chinense*, belonging to the habanero family, not *C. baccatum*.

The aji originated in the area that is today northern Bolivia and Southern

C. Baccatum Flower.

(Opposite page) Assortment of Aji fruits.

Peru and, according to archaeological evidence, was domesticated about 4,500 BCE. Archaeological evidence shows that the species was gradually improved by pre-Incan civilizations. Fruit size increased and fruits gradually became nondeciduous, meaning they remained on the plant through ripening. The peppers were depicted in Inca times in drawings and pottery, and recent archaeological diggings have found extensive *C. baccatum* plant material at the Huaca Prieta archaeological site in Peru. Today, ajis are grown from southern Brazil to Bolivia, Ecuador, Peru, and Chile.

Aji Amarillo

The Aji Amarillo is often called Escabeche (es-kah-BECH-ay) because it is the chile pepper used to make this marinated seafood dish. The Aji Amarillo is the chile pepper of choice to season ceviche, wherein one "cooks" the seafood in an acidic sauce and serves it cold. The Aji Amarillo is among the most widely grown in Peru and is used daily in all Peruvian dishes either as a sauce on the plate or as an ingredient (often a paste) in dishes. It has a unique spicy, full-bodied, fruity flavor with a delayed heat. The fruit is a bright orange pepper with a thick flesh and a medium-to-high heat level. Aji Amarillo are used fresh but are often seen in international markets in a canned, paste, or dried form. They can be used dried as the flavor becomes more concentrated and lightly sweeter, reminding one of raisins or sun-dried tomatoes. Plus, once dried, they keep for years. And if you are taking a deep breath and pondering the idea of adding yet another chile pepper to your kitchen repertoire, know that the Aji Amarillo has a different taste from most other widely used chile peppers.

Causa Rellena (Layered Potato Dish)

This traditional Peruvian layered dish is made with potatoes and chicken salad. It is served cold and can be an appetizer or a light meal. The potatoes can also be molded or cut into circles to create a type of potato sandwich with the chicken salad in the middle.

INSTRUCTIONS

Peel, cook, and mash the potatoes. Mix the potatoes with the chile, salt, and juice from half a lemon. Knead until ingredients form a well-mixed paste. If the potatoes don't stick together well, add a tiny amount of oil and continue kneading until they stick. In a separate container, season the onion with salt and juice from half a lemon. Then shred the chicken and mix it with half the mayonnaise. Separate the potato and chile mixture into portions and add the chicken on top of each portion. Place the Causa Rellena on a lettuce leaf and top with the remaining mayonnaise and parsley. Serves 4.

INGREDIENTS

2 lbs. yellow potatoes

1 cup Aji Amarillo chiles (minced)

1 tsp. salt

1 lemon

1 small onion (chopped)

1 large skinless chicken breast (cooked)

1 cup light or fat free mayonnaise

Lettuce leaves

Parsley

Capsicum baccatum

Amarillo Ceviche

Ceviche is the best-known of all Peruvian dishes. Aji Amarillo chile pepper adds a flavorful blend to the raw fish and is a traditional ceviche staple. At Paul Bosland's home there is a tradition called the "hot luck," in which his students bring a dish to share that is a family specialty. Unless there is a Peruvian invited to the hot luck, Paul will prepare ceviche. A firm fish like halibut or cod is good but feel free to substitute bay scallops or shrimp, or even make a mix of all three.

INSTRUCTIONS

Combine the fish and enough lime juice to cover in a bowl. Allow to marinate in the refrigerator for 20 minutes. Drain the fish, reserving ¼ cup of lime juice. Combine the fish with reserved lime juice, onion, cilantro, Aji Amarillo chile pepper, jalapeno, ginger, olive oil, and Aji Amarillo paste and season to taste with salt. Stir gently to combine. Chill thoroughly. To serve, garnish with tortilla chips and slices of avocado. Serves 4.

INGREDIENTS

1 lb. skinless, boneless sustainable firm fish such as halibut (cut into ¼-inch pieces)

1 cup lime juice (freshly squeezed)

½ red onion (diced)

½ bunch cilantro (chopped)

1 Aji Amarillo chile pepper (deveined, deseeded, and minced)

1 jalapeno (deveined, deseeded, and diced)

½ inch piece of fresh ginger (peeled and minced)

4 tbsps. extra virgin olive oil

1½ tsps. Aji Amarillo paste

Salt to taste

Plantain chips *or* tortilla chips, for garnish

Sliced avocado, for garnish

Aji Limon

Aji Limon (also called Aji Lemon Drop) gets its name from the bright green-to-yellow color of its fruit. Its fabulous flavor has lots of fruit overtones, with a note of citrus. The pod is crinkled and cone shaped, measuring about 3 to 4 inches long and ½ inch wide. It has a distinctive fruity flavor and is used in fresh salsas or dried and ground into a beautiful powder.

Aji Limon fruits.

Mexican Street Corn

INGREDIENTS

4 ears sweet corn (husks removed)

2 tbsps. butter (melted)

1 tsp. chipotle chile powder

½ cup mayonnaise

1 tbsp. fresh lime juice

1 tbsp. cilantro (finely chopped)

½ tsp. salt

1½ cups Mexican cheeses (blended together and finely shredded)

1 avocado (pitted and diced)

¼ cup red bell pepper (diced)

¼ cup red onion (diced)

1 Aji Limon pepper (deveined, deseeded, and diced)

½ tsp. kosher salt

Black pepper, to taste

¼ tsp. cumin

1 lime wedge (optional)

In this delicious recipe, sweet corn is brushed with a chipotle chile butter, then grilled, cut off the cob, and tossed with a shredded blend of Mexican cheeses, mayonnaise, lime juice, cilantro, and salt, topped with a diced avocado, bell pepper, and onion.

INSTRUCTIONS

Preheat grill. Transfer the corn to a plate and brush the ears with melted butter. Sprinkle each with chile powder. Transfer to a plate. Grill the corn over medium heat in a closed grill for 10 to 15 minutes or until lightly charred, rotating the corn as it cooks. Remove from the grill and set aside to cool. In a medium bowl, combine the mayonnaise, lime juice, cilantro, and salt. Stir in the cheese. Cut the corn off the cob with a sharp knife and transfer into the bowl containing the mayonnaise, lime juice cilantro, and cheese mixture. Stir to combine. In another medium bowl, combine the remaining ingredients except the lime wedge. Spoon the grilled corn salad into a bowl or serving dish and top with the avocado mixture. Sprinkle red chile powder over top for color and taste. Squeeze the wedge of lime over salad and serve. The salad can be warmed in the oven until the cheese has melted and served with the cold avocado mixture spooned on top. Serves 3.

Devil Salt

Use this sassy recipe to put the finishing touches on chicken, hard-boiled eggs, your favorite meat, or fish.

INSTRUCTIONS

Wearing gloves, make a pile of all the ingredients except the salt on a cutting board and finely chop and mash together with the side of your knife until a nice paste forms. Add the paste and the salt to a bowl and mix together thoroughly. Add more salt, if desired. Store in the refrigerator for up to 2 weeks.

INGREDIENTS

3 Aji Amarillos or any floral hot pepper (deveined, deseeded, and finely chopped)

3 Aji Limon peppers (deveined, deseeded, and finely chopped)

1 garlic clove (finely grated)

One 1-inch piece fresh ginger (finely grated)

1 tbsp. yuzu juice *or* lemon juice

Zest of 1 orange

Zest of 1 grapefruit

Zest of 1 lime

1 cup kosher salt

Capsicum baccatum

Omnicolor

This beautifully stunning hot variety provides a useful inimitable spicy fruit with the added benefit that it gradually changes colors from yellow with a violet overtone to light orange to dark orange to red-orange and then finally to red. In the Teaching Garden, you may notice the immature pale-yellow fruits turn a translucent purplish blush when the Garden has a number of strong sunlit days: this is the chile pepper's natural defense against UV radiation. Ripening occurs over a long period, so at any one time the plant can be covered in a rainbow of different colored fruits. The pods can be harvested at any stage depending on the intended use. Pods measure up to 2½ inches by ½ inch and grow upright and outward on 2-foot-high plants. Plants look attractive in hanging baskets as their branches grow up and out approximately 2 feet by 4 feet, for a broad, full spread.

Aji Omnicolor Peruvian Sauce

Enjoy the flavor notes in this traditional sauce on your favorite meat, fish, or poultry dish.

INSTRUCTIONS

Put the ajis, onion, and garlic in a medium frying pan over medium heat with enough oil to cover the bottom of the pan. Add the black pepper, oregano, and cumin. Continue to stir all these ingredients as they sweat in the frying pan for about 8 to 10 minutes in order to help bring out their flavors. Once you take the pan off the heat, let it sit until the contents are relatively cool. This may take 20 to 30 minutes. After your ingredients have cooled put them into a blender with a little bit of added water to help the mixing process and then add the salt. Finally, turn on the blender and watch as your ingredients turn into the delicious aji sauce. Try it over rotisserie chicken. Yields 4 servings.

INGREDIENTS

3 to 6 Aji Omnicolor peppers (deveined, deseeded, and finely chopped)

1 large onion (chopped)

1 clove of garlic (minced)

¼ tbsp. black pepper

¼ tbsp. oregano

¼ tbsp. cumin

1 tbsp. salt

Enough oil to fry ingredients

Chicken, Fennel, and Pepper Pizza

Fennel has a licorice or anise flavor and adds a mild, but not over-powering, flavor to this dish. Coriander compliments the fennel and lends a flavorful and not-so-traditional twist to this chicken pizza recipe. Use your favorite pizza dough and enjoy.

INSTRUCTIONS

Preheat oven to 450°F. Heat the oil in a large nonstick skillet over medium heat. Add the fennel, bell peppers, and Aji Omnicolor pepper and cook until vegetables begin to soften. Add the cut chicken and coriander and continue cooking until chicken is cooked through. Top the pizza dough with the chicken and fennel mixture, spreading evenly over the crust. Add the cheeses and top with ground pepper. Bake in the oven until the cheese melts and turns golden brown, 10 to 15 minutes. Sprinkle with chopped fennel as soon as the pizza is removed from the oven. Serves 4.

INGREDIENTS

2 tsps. olive oil

1 bulb fennel (quartered, cored, and thinly sliced, plus 1 tbsp. chopped feathery tops for garnish)

1 red bell pepper (thinly sliced)

2 tsps. finely chopped or powdered Aji Omnicolor pepper

8 oz. boneless, skinless chicken breast (very thinly sliced crosswise)

1 tsp. ground coriander

¾ cup part skim mozzarella cheese (grated)

¼ cup parmesan cheese (grated)

Freshly ground pepper, to taste

Capsicum baccatum

Bishop's Crown/ Christmas Bell

Few chile peppers have as distinctive a look as the bishop's crown pepper. The fruit is typically about 2 inches wide and 1 inch tall. Its shape is unique, reminiscent of the miters worn by Catholic bishops. The distinctive look has provided a slew of additional names for this chile pepper: Christmas bell, joker's hat, orchid, and balloon chile pepper, to name a few. All, of course, are just as fitting for the shape. They're also known as piri-piri in some regions. The fruits go from green to red. It's surprisingly versatile in the kitchen, too, with a large cavity (relative to its small size) that's ideal for stuffing. Overall, these peppers have a medium heat, comparable to the heat level of a jalapeno. The green to red pods are eaten fresh or pickled and are sometimes strung up as a tree garland.

INGREDIENTS

Dressing

1 cup olive oil

1 cup white vinegar

¼ tsp. horseradish

1⅓ cups sugar

2 tbsps. salt

2 tbsps. celery seed

¾ tsp. black pepper

¼ tsp. white pepper

Salad

2 lbs. green cabbage (chopped and shredded)

1 lb. red cabbage (chopped and shredded)

1 Christmas bell pepper (deveined, deseeded, and finely chopped)

2 green bell peppers (deveined, deseeded, and finely chopped)

1 large onion (diced)

1 carrot (grated)

Spanish Cole Slaw

If you're looking for a favorite new coleslaw recipe, we're sure you'll like this one.

INSTRUCTIONS

Combine the first 8 ingredients in a saucepan. Boil rapidly for 1 minute. Allow to cool for 5 minutes. Combine the 6 salad ingredients in a large serving bowl. Mix the dressing thoroughly and pour over salad ingredients. Refrigerate for several hours before serving. Serves 8 to 10.

Cucumber Pepper Soup

If you've planted a vine or two of cucumbers in your kitchen garden, this recipe will excite your palate and fill your kitchen with a whole-hearted fragrance. Using fresh ingredients whenever possible will only serve to enhance the blend of flavors.

INSTRUCTIONS

Place a medium-sized soup pot on the stove. Add the butter and melt it on medium heat. Fry the cucumber slices and garlic for 2 to 3 minutes. Add the vegetable stock and half of both the bishop's crown pepper and jalapeno pepper (if you are using it). Cover the pot and turn the stove to simmer. Let the ingredients simmer for 15 minutes. Pour the simmered ingredients into a food processor. Blend until the ingredients are smooth. Pour them back into the soup pot. Add the fresh cream and dill, cover again, and let the soup simmer for another 5 minutes. Add salt to taste. Top with bacon bits or paprika. Serve immediately as the first dinner course or as the main dish with fresh rolls or bread. Serves 3.

INGREDIENTS

1 tsp. butter

2 large fresh cucumbers (skinned and sliced)

3 cloves of garlic (finely chopped)

2 cups vegetable stock

1 jalapeno pepper (destemmed, deseeded, and sliced into strips or chopped, optional)

1 bishop's crown pepper (destemmed, deseeded, and sliced into strips or chopped)

1 cup fresh cream

1 tbsp. fresh dill leaves (finely chopped)

Salt to taste

2 bacon slices (cooked and chopped into tiny pieces, optional)

Paprika (optional)

Capsicum chinense

T he last domesticated species in the Teaching Garden is *C. chinense*. The *C. chinense* species, like all *Capsicum* species, originated in the Western Hemisphere. This species originated in the Amazon Basin and from there made its way around the West Indies via Native Americans who took seeds with them when they traveled to explore neighboring islands. Eventually each island would grow their own pod type that would in time become specifically adapted to that island. These pods are a good example of "landraces," all related but varying slightly in shape, color, and heat profile. This species is now the most cultivated and most highly esteemed of the chile peppers in the Caribbean region. The most common chile peppers in the Caribbean are the habanero, rocotillo, and the Scotch bonnet. Habanero may be the best-known pod type of this species, but the diversity in fruit shape in this species is great. Fruit can be extremely hot with a persistent heat when eaten. This species has the distinction of including the hottest chile peppers in the world. On the other end of the spectrum, there is even a no-heat cultivar, NuMex Trick-or-Treat. *C. chinense* is used to flavor many different dishes and cuisines worldwide and often used in hot sauces and condiments. The species compliments seafood dishes and pairs well with citrus. A key way to tell *C. chinense* from *C. annuum* in the Teaching Garden is that the *C. chinense* plants set two to six fruits per node.

Habanero

The name "habanero" describes a specific pod type from the Yucatan Peninsula of Mexico, even though the name refers to Havana, Cuba. Today, it refers to a pod type that is lantern-shaped, is orange or red at maturity, and is very hot. In fact, Dominican priest Francisco Ximenez wrote of the habanero in 1722 that a single pod would "make a bull unable to eat." But they can be milder. For example, types grown in the Teaching Garden include the mild NuMex Suave (orange and red) and NuMex Trick-or-Treat, a no-heat habanero. The fruits are used fresh in salsas, cooked directly in dishes, or fermented to make hot sauce.

(Opposite page)
Habanero peppers. Image courtesy of Acton Crawford, liscened under CC 2.0.

Spanish Shrimp Tapas

Shrimp tapas are a popular appetizer in Spain. You can use fresh or frozen shrimp, peeled and deveined or with the tail on—whatever you prefer. If you are using frozen shrimp, be sure to allow shrimp to thaw for about ten minutes before you cook with them.

INSTRUCTIONS

Add the garlic and just enough water to cover it to a small bowl. Let sit for 5 to 10 minutes, then drain excess water. Thaw the shrimp and rinse in cold water and pat dry. In a small bowl, mix the chile pepper powder, nutmeg, and sugar. Heat the olive oil in a cast iron skillet to medium-high heat. Add the garlic and cook for 2 to 3 minutes, being careful not to brown. Remove the garlic from the pan and set aside. Turn the heat to high. Season the shrimp with salt and pepper. Add the shrimp to the pan and sear each side for about 1 minute. When the shrimp becomes pink and has some sear marks, toss in the dry spice mixture and ½ of the parsley. Cook for about 30 seconds to warm the spices. Remove from heat and serve immediately with lemon slices on the side. Use the rest of the parsley as garnish. Serves 6.

INGREDIENTS

1½ tsps. garlic cloves (minced)

21 to 25 *or* 1 lb. shrimp (peeled and deveined)

1 tbsp. red habanero powder

½ tsp. ground nutmeg

¼ tsp. sugar

⅓ cup olive oil

¼ tsp. salt

½ tsp. ground black pepper

¼ cup fresh parsley (chopped)

1 lemon (quartered)

Dukkah Flatbread

This Egyptian flat bread is a favorite eaten for break-fast, as a snack, or dipped in olive oil and served as an appetizer. After locating the Dukkah spice (a blend of spices, nuts, and herbs), which is commonly sold in several grocery outlets, you will also discover several other uses for the spice blend, such as a topping for yogurt oatmeal.

INSTRUCTIONS

In a small bowl, stir together ½ cup of the milk warmed to between 110°F to 115°F, yeast, and sugar. Let stand for about 5 minutes until the mixture starts to foam. In a large bowl, stir together the flour and salt. Add the yogurt, butter, chopped chile pepper, remaining warm milk, and yeast mixture. Slowly fold the ingredients together to combine until the dough forms into a ball. Lightly dust a work surface with flour and knead the ball of dough for about 5 minutes. The dough should be lightly tacky but you can add a little more flour if the dough is really sticky. Continue kneading until the dough is smooth and transfer it to a bowl. Cover the bowl with a towel and let rest in a warm place for about 1 hour. The dough should double in size. After 1 hour, preheat the oven to 450°F. If you are using a pizza stone or stone baking sheet, you

INGREDIENTS

1 cup milk

1 packet or 2 tsps. active dry yeast

1 tsp. sugar

2¼ cups whole wheat white flour, plus some extra for dusting the work surface

1 tsp. salt

3 tbsps. Greek yogurt, plain and unsweetened

1 NuMex Trick-or-Treat (deseeded, destemmed, and finely chopped)

2 tbsps. butter (melted)

2 tbsps. olive oil

2 tbsps. Dukkah spice mix

Cooking spray

can place it in the oven to heat also. If using a traditional baking sheet, spray with cooking spray to prevent the bread from sticking. Punch down the dough and transfer to a lightly floured work surface. Divide the dough into 6 equal pieces and roll each piece into an oval shape, about 8 inches x 5 inches. Carefully, transfer the bread to the hot pizza stone (you may have to work in 2 batches) and bake about 5 minutes or until the bread starts to brown and bubbles form on the top. With tongs, carefully turn the bread and bake for another 3 to 4 minutes. If you are using a traditional baking sheet, you may need a minute or two longer in the oven because the baking sheet was not preheated. Remove the warm bread from the oven and lightly brush each piece with olive oil. Sprinkle the Dukkah blend on the bread and serve warm. Serves 6.

NuMex Suave Orange/Red

NuMex Suave Orange and NuMex Suave Red were the first mild commercial habaneros to be introduced. The name "Suave" comes from the Spanish for "mellow" or "smooth," to emphasize the mild nature of these chile peppers. The pods are significantly less hot that normal habaneros. NuMex Suave Orange is at 835 SHUs and NuMex Suave Red is at a smooth 580 SHUs. This is less than 1 percent of the heat of the standard commercial Orange Habanero. Why breed a mild habanero? Habaneros have unique flavors, but most people are afraid to taste them because they're so hot. Now people can taste these exotic flavors without being afraid of setting their mouths on fire. The NuMex Suave habaneros have a citrusy flavor with an orange-lemony overtone. You'll feel a sensation of heat in the back of your throat, as opposed to a jalapeno where you'll feel the heat on the tip of your tongue and lips.

(Opposite page)
NuMex Suave
Habaneros.

Suave Fish Tacos

Presented here is a combination of three sets of ingredients for a weekend afternoon lunch on the deck or patio. While the barbeque is heating up, enjoy a favorite beverage with chips and salsa, leaving enough room for these tasty tacos.

INSTRUCTIONS

Mix the achiote, lime juice, olive oil, garlic, cumin, and salt. Rub the mixture on both sides of the fish. Place fish in a container with a lid and cover tightly, then refrigerate for 2 hours. Preheat grill, brush the fish with olive oil and grill for 4 minutes on each side for medium-well. Fills 10 to 12 taco shells.

INGREDIENTS

Three 8–oz. snapper fillets *or* your favorite fresh fish (white fish varieties are recommended)

10 to 12 fresh taco shells

Fish Rub:

2 tbsps. achiote paste

4 tbsps. lime juice

2 tbsps. olive oil

4 cloves garlic, finely chopped

1 tsp. cumin

1 tsp. salt

Capsicum chinense

INGREDIENTS

4 small ripe tomatoes (chopped)

¼ cup red onion (minced)

2 tbsps. cilantro (chopped)

2 tbsps. parsley (chopped)

2 cloves garlic (finely chopped)

¼ tsp. ground cumin

2 tsps. fresh lime juice

1 tbsp. suave habanero pepper (destemmed, deseeded, and finely chopped)

Bag of tortilla chips

Suave Salsa

This salsa can be made a few days ahead of time by mixing all ingredients together and refrigerating them. Enjoy the citrusy flavor the habanero brings to the salsa!

INSTRUCTIONS

Mix all ingredients together by hand, cover, and place in the refrigerator. Prep the fish for the tacos, and, when placing the rubbed fish in the refrigerator, take the salsa out so you can entertain your guests while they wait for the barbecue. Let salsa warm to room temperature before serving.

Chicken Quesadillas

Feel free to dial this recipe up or down, depending on your guests. Whether you are gearing up for the big game with the family or just dinner at home for two, this recipe is sure to be a big hit.

INGREDIENTS

2 tbsps. extra virgin olive oil

2 garlic cloves (minced)

1 lb. boneless skinless chicken breast (thinly sliced)

½ tsp. ground paprika

1 tsp. fresh lime juice

1 to 2 NuMex Suave chile peppers (deveined, destemmed, roasted, peeled, and sliced)

Kosher or sea salt, to taste

Fresh cracked black pepper, to taste

6 oz. cheddar cheese (grated)

Eight 8-inch flour tortillas

Salsa, guacamole, and sour cream (optional)

INSTRUCTIONS

Heat a large skillet over medium-high heat. Add the oil and stir in the garlic. Cook until soft and then add the chicken, paprika, lime juice, and chile peppers. Cook the chicken for about 3 to 5 minutes or until cooked through. Season with salt and pepper and remove from the heat. Set aside. Spread half of the cheese on 4 tortillas. Top with the NuMex Suave chicken. Add a final layer of cheese and gently spread the filling evenly around the tortilla, leaving a gap around the edges. Top with the remaining tortillas. Heat a large skillet or griddle over medium-high heat. Place a filled tortilla in the pan and cook for about 3 minutes or until the bottom is golden. Carefully flip the quesadilla and cook for another 2 to 3 minutes until the second side is golden and the cheese is completely melted. Remove from the pan and repeat with the remaining quesadillas. Allow each to cool for a few minutes before cutting into 4 to 6 pieces with a pizza slicer. Serve with salsa, guacamole and/or sour cream, as desired. Serves 4 to 6.

NuMex Trick-or-Treat

NuMex Trick-or-Treat is a no-heat habanero. NuMex Trick-or-Treat has an orange lantern-shaped pod reminiscent of the Orange Habanero. The name, NuMex-Trick-or-Treat, is a play on words because the Orange Habanero from the Yucatan is very hot with a heat level of greater than 150,000 SHUs, while NuMex Trick-or-Treat has no heat, that is, zero SHUs. The lack of heat in a chile pepper fruit can occur in two ways. One is the inability of the plant to make the capsaicinoids, the determinants of chile pepper heat. Another method is for the fruit to lack the vesicles in the fruit that allow for the capsaicinoids to be produced. The lack of heat in the fruit of NuMex Trick-or-Treat is associated with the Loss of Vesicles (*lov*) gene.

Turkey Lime Soup

Use this recipe when you are faced with turkey leftovers. It's a version of the lime soup that originates from the Yucatan peninsula of Mexico. But this version has a bit of a twist. The toppings really make this soup great, so don't skimp on the lime wedges, scallions, chile peppers, and/or avocado.

INSTRUCTIONS

Combine first four ingredients in a Dutch oven over medium-high heat; bring to a simmer. Cover and cook 30 minutes. Strain the broth through a colander into a bowl; discard solids.

Return the broth to the pan; stir in the turkey, cilantro, and lime juice. Cook over low heat for 5 minutes or until thoroughly heated. Garnish with lime wedges, scallions, crushed or powdered peppers, and/or avocados. Serves 4.

INGREDIENTS

12 garlic gloves, crushed

Four 4.5–oz. cans of fat-free, low sodium chicken broth

2 garlic cloves, whole

2 large onions (trimmed and quartered)

3 cups chopped and skinned cooked turkey

¼ cup fresh cilantro

¼ cup fresh lime juice

1 fresh lime (cut into wedges)

1 small bunch scallions (chopped)

1 NuMex Trick–or–Treat chile pepper (dried, destemmed, deseeded, and crushed or powdered)

1 avocado (sliced)

INGREDIENTS

1 lb. of beef top sirloin steak (cut into thin strips)

1 tbsp. fresh ginger (minced)

3 garlic cloves (minced)

¼ tsp. pepper

¾ tsp. salt

1 cup light coconut milk

2 tbsps. sugar

1 tbsp. sriracha chile pepper sauce

½ tsp. grated lime zest

2 tbsps. lime juice

2 tbsps. canola oil

1 red bell pepper (cut into thin strips)

½ red onion (thinly sliced)

1 NuMex Trick–or–Treat fresh pepper (thinly sliced)

4 cups fresh baby spinach

2 cups green onions (thinly sliced)

2 tbsps. fresh cilantro (chopped)

Spicy Stir Fry

For those who enjoy the taste of a good cut of beef, this stir-fry recipe combines your vegetables and meat for a full plate of healthful enjoyment.

INSTRUCTIONS

In a large bowl, toss the beef with the ginger, 2 garlic cloves, pepper, and ½ teaspoon salt; let stand 15 minutes. In a small bowl, whisk together the coconut milk, sugar, chile pepper sauce, lime zest, lime juice, and remaining salt until blended. In a large skillet, heat 1 tablespoon oil over medium-high heat. Add the beef; stir-fry until no longer pink, 2 to 3 minutes. Remove from the pan. Stir-fry the bell pepper, red onion, NuMex Trick-or-Treat pepper, and remaining garlic in remaining oil just until the vegetables are crisp-tender, 2 to 3 minutes. Stir in the coconut milk mixture, heat through. Add the spinach and beef; cook until the spinach is wilted and the beef is heated through, stirring occasionally. Sprinkle with green onions and cilantro. Serves 4.

Fisheye

What makes this *Capsicum chinense* chile pepper plant distinctive is its small, round-shaped fruits that look very much like a chiltepin, or a "fisheye." Its fruits change from green to yellow orange. Fisheye plants can produce 170 to 180 pods per season; in a tropical climate, they can produce up to three crops a year. Fisheye fruits are extremely aromatic and hot! The fruits are used to season fresh seafood but are also used in sauces and can be pickled.

Fisheye pepper plant (courtesy of Amy Goldman Fowler).

Fisheye Hot Sauce

This hot sauce is a fine balance of sweetness and heat. It combines the sweetness of pineapple and the heat and flavor from the peppers. It can be served fresh—no cooking needed—just blend all the ingredients and serve.

INSTRUCTIONS

Add all the ingredients to a pan over medium high heat. Simmer for 10 minutes—until the chile peppers and onions are soft. Let the mixture cool to room temperature, then blend in a food processor until smooth. The sauce is often served thick and chunky—no need to strain.

INGREDIENTS

4 to 5 fisheye peppers

¼ cup onion (chopped)

½ cup fresh pineapple

3 garlic cloves (chopped)

¼ cup white vinegar

1 tsp. mustard

1 tbsp. honey

1 tsp. salt

2 tbsps. cilantro

Caldo de Piranha (Fish Soup)

We didn't believe it until we tried this recipe for the first time. Piranha has a delicious flavor, which becomes even more pleasing with the fisheye peppers. This may require a trip to Peru but try it!

INGREDIENTS

4 lbs. piranhas or any small fresh-water fish (e.g., perch, walleye, pike)

3 garlic cloves (minced)

3 tbsps. fresh-squeezed lime juice

1 tbsp. white wine *or* cider vinegar

Salt and pepper to taste

½ cup plus 2 tbsps. vegetable oil

5 fisheye peppers (deveined, destemmed, and cut in half)

2 large tomatoes (peeled, deseeded, and chopped)

1 large green bell pepper (cut into julienne strips)

1 medium onion (chopped)

1 tbsp. green onion (chopped)

2 tbsps. cilantro (chopped)

INSTRUCTIONS

Clean and descale the fish, then cut into large chunks. Place the fish chunks in a large bowl and season with the garlic, lime juice, vinegar, and salt and pepper to taste. Let marinate in the refrigerator for approximately 2 hours. In a large saucepan, heat ½ cup of oil over medium-high heat. Add the chunks of piranha and stir-fry for a few minutes. Lower the heat, then add boiling water to cover the fish and bring to a boil. Cover and cook for 10 minutes or until the fish is tender. Add fisheye peppers to the broth. Remove from heat, then using a strainer remove the fish from the broth, reserving both. Let the fish cool. Once cool enough to handle, carefully remove all bones from the pieces of fish. Place the fish pieces and the reserved broth in a blender or food processor and blend until you have a smooth mixture. Reserve. In another saucepan, heat the 2 tablespoons oil over medium-high heat. Add the tomatoes, green pepper strips, and chopped onion and cook until the onions are transparent and all ingredients are softened. Add the piranha broth to the pan, then the chopped green onion and cilantro. Heat thoroughly. Serves 8.

Cajamarca

Cajamarca has a tantalizing pod color transition. It is as appealing to the eye as it is to eat. The fruit starts as a vibrant purple unique to *C. chinense* and matures to a rich red. The wonderful fragrant aroma of the Cajamarca captures attention with its intense, spicy citrus fragrance and the classic habanero fruity undertone. It has a delayed heat characteristic of *C. chinense*; the heat level is in the medium range. The plants have semiglossy foliage and grow into a tall, upright bush generously loaded with fruits that will provide a bountiful harvest all summer. The fruit shape and size are much like the regular orange habanero: wrinkled, 1 inch to 1½ inches long, resembling a Chinese lantern with a tapered end. They are collected in the marketplace of the city of Cajamarca, the capital of the region by the same name and the most important city of the Northern Andes Mountain range in Peru. This region also expands into the Amazon Rainforest, where the Cajamarca originates. Peruvians remember Cajamarca as the place that marked the defeat of the Inca Empire by Spanish invaders, as the Incan emperor Atahualpa was captured and murdered there. Cajamarca has been designated an American Heritage Site by UNESCO.

(Opposite page) Cajamarca fruit color transitions.

235

Sudado

Sudado is a simple northern Peruvian fish stew recipe with tomatoes, red onion, and chile peppers that is very typical of northern Peruvian cuisine. The intense lime tang brings depth that really makes this an outstanding dish. Maintaining the tradition requires boiled yucca and rice to be served alongside!

INSTRUCTIONS

In a large bowl marinate the fish in the lime juice, cilantro, salt, and pepper. Puree the chopped chile peppers and ½ cup water in a blender until smooth. Set aside. Heat oil in a large skillet over medium-high heat. Add the garlic and cook until fragrant (about 30 seconds). Carefully add the pureed pepperoncini chile peppers and cook for 2 minutes. Add the onions and cook until soft, about 5 minutes. Add the fish and marinade along with 1½ cups hot water and stir liquid gently to combine. Top the filets evenly with the four Cajamarca chile peppers and tomatoes and sprinkle with oregano. Reduce heat to medium-low and simmer, covered, until the fish is cooked (about 15 minutes). Season with salt and pepper to taste. Place the fish in individual bowls and top with liquid. Serves 4.

INGREDIENTS

2 lbs. mild-flavored white fish filet (deboned and skinless)

2 tbsps. fresh lime juice

2 tbsps. fresh cilantro (chopped)

2 tsps. salt

1 tsp. freshly ground black pepper

2 cups water

8 pepperoncini chile peppers (chopped)

4 Cajamarca chile peppers (deveined, deseeded, and thinly sliced)

¼ cup canola oil

4 garlic cloves (mashed to a paste)

1 medium red onion (halved and cut into ½ inch slices)

2 large plum tomatoes (cored, deseeded, and coarsely chopped)

1 tsp. dried oregano (lightly toasted)

Cajamarca Sauce

You will find yourself adding this tasty Peruvian sauce to many of your favorite dishes, so consider doubling the recipe the second time you make it.

INSTRUCTIONS

Combine the Cajamarca pods, green onions, sweet onion, and cilantro in processor; puree until paste forms, scraping down the sides of the blender with a rubber spatula several times. Add 2 tablespoons vinegar and process until the mixture is blended but some texture remains. Transfer to a small bowl. Stir in salt, pepper, and more vinegar, if desired. Can be made 1 day ahead. Cover and refrigerate. Yields enough to serve 1 meal.

INGREDIENTS

½ cup Cajamarca pods (deveined, deseeded, and coarsely chopped)

½ cup green onions (coarsely chopped)

⅓ cup sweet onion (coarsely chopped)

¼ cup fresh cilantro (coarsely chopped)

2 tbsps. (or more) red wine vinegar *or* fresh lime juice

¾ tsp. coarse kosher salt

¼ tsp. freshly ground black pepper

Scotch Bonnet

Asking for a hot chile pepper in most of the Caribbean islands gets you the Scotch bonnet chile pepper. Scotch bonnet is used in all sorts of Caribbean cuisine, including the well-known jerk chicken or jerk pork. The shape of this famous pepper is what inspired its name. The fruit has a squashed look that resembles a Scotsman's bonnet (Tam O'Shanter hat). Scotch bonnet is also known as Bonney, Bahama Mama, Jamaican Hot, Bahamian, Martinique, or Caribbean red peppers. Most Scotch bonnets are hot, having a heat rating of 100,000 to 350,000 SHUs. In 2002 the Scotch bonnet was recognized as one of Jamaica's competitive nontraditional export crops. It can be eaten raw with a meal, boiled in a pot of soup, cooked in rice and beans, or used to make seasonings for meat, including jerk. The Scotch bonnet is distinct from the habanero, for which it is often confused. Fresh, ripe Scotch bonnet fruit changes from green as it matures, usually to yellow, white, red, or orange. A chocolate color is rare. They can be found at US supermarkets, especially in areas high in Caribbean residents. The fruit have a slightly sweet taste to them, sort of like a tomato with a slight hint of apples and cherries.

Jamaican Chicken Curry and Potatoes

This flavorful chicken dish is easy to make, and the curry powder adds beauty to its presentation.

INSTRUCTIONS

Heat the oil in a medium-sized saucepot at a medium heat. Add the onions, ginger, and Scotch bonnet pepper. Sauté for 5 to 8 minutes. Add the butter and curry powder and let sit until the curry powder turns a dark gold. Add the chicken and continue to cook for 8 to 10 minutes. Add the potatoes and cook for another couple of minutes before adding the coconut milk and chicken stock. Let simmer for 30 to 45 minutes. Serves 6 to 8.

INGREDIENTS

4 tbsps. olive oil

1 yellow onion (chopped)

1 tsp. fresh ginger (minced)

1 small Scotch bon-net pepper (deveined, deseeded, and minced)

½ stick butter

2 tbsps. Jamaican curry powder

1½ lbs. chicken breasts (cooked and chopped into 1–inch pieces)

2 large russet potatoes (chopped)

One 16-oz. can coconut milk

8 oz. chicken stock

Jerk Burger

These burgers can be quite hot if you use fresh Scotch bonnet peppers. If you prefer a little less heat but want to maintain the flavor, buy jerk seasoning or make the jerk sauce recipe listed under the section on rocotillo peppers. It usually contains Scotch bonnet pepper but in a much smaller quantity.

INSTRUCTIONS

Mix all ingredients in a large bowl. Form patties and grill over medium coals until desired degree of doneness. Serve on hoagie rolls. Serves 3 to 4.

INGREDIENTS:

3 tbsps. jerk seasoning *or* 1 small Scotch bonnet pepper (deveined, deseeded, and minced)

3 tbsps. orange juice

2 tbsps. lime juice

2 tbsps. apple cider vinegar

1 tbsp. soy sauce

1 lb. ground beef

Datil

It is thought that the datil pepper was introduced into the United States via trade with the Caribbean islanders. However, David Nolan of St. Augustine, Florida, wrote that "it was brought to St. Augustine about 1880 from Chile by a jelly manufacturer named S. B. Valls." This was the first reference to datil peppers being observed in the United States. Nolan believes the datil was adopted by St. Augustine's Minorcan residents as part of their cuisine. Furthermore, he says that *datil* is a Spanish word meaning "date"; it is also a word in the Quechua language of the Inca Empire.

Datil pepper fruits grow to 4 inches long, maturing from green to a yellowish-orange color when ripe. Many people utilize the datil pepper in their recipes in order to add some kick to their Minorcan chowder or other local dishes. A datil pepper is similar in its heat index to a habanero (100,000 to 300,000 SHUs). But unlike habaneros, datil peppers are sweet with a fruitful tangy taste to them. Although datil peppers can be found outside St. Augustine, it is very rare, and a majority of the datil pepper products sold on the market today are grown in and around St. Augustine because datil peppers need warm growing conditions. Datil is commonly used to make relishes, hot sauces, or dried flakes to spice up a dish or as a salt substitute.

Datil Pepper Jelly

This jelly can be used on toast in the morning to wake up the senses or with cheese and crackers in the evening on the back patio with a spritzer.

INSTRUCTIONS

Remove seeds from the bell pepper and grind the bells in a food processor. Save the juice and mix with vinegar and sugar. Bring to a full boil for about 7 minutes. Add the ground datil pepper and cook for 2 minutes. Cool for 5 minutes, then add the Certo. Bring to a full rolling boil for about 2 minutes, then cool 5 minutes. Skim and pour into sterilized jelly jars. Yields twelve ½-pint jars.

INGREDIENTS

1¾ cups sweet bell pepper (ground)

½ cup juice from bell pepper

1 cup apple cider vinegar

11 cups sugar

½ cup datil pepper (ground)

2 twin-packs of Certo

Twelve ½-pint jelly jars and lids (sterilized)

Jamaican Style Greens

To enjoy your fresh garden produce while experimenting with the flavors of your pepper crop, use one datil pepper or substitute a small cayenne or two serrano peppers for less heat.

INSTRUCTIONS

Clean, destem, and wash the greens. Steam the spinach in a pot over medium heat with the water that is clinging to the spinach. Cook until the leaves wilt (which will happen quickly). Place the remaining wet greens in a second pot and cook until the leaves wilt. Heat the oil in a skillet and sauté the onion over medium heat for about 5 minutes. Roughly chop all the greens, keeping the spinach separate from the other greens. Add all greens except the spinach to the skillet with the pepper and allspice. Cover and cook over a low heat until the kale, collards, and chard are tender. Then add the spinach, which will take only a few moments to become tender. Add salt and pepper and serve hot. Serves 4 to 6.

INGREDIENTS

1 to 2 lbs. greens (recommend kale, spinach, collards, and chard)

1 tbsp. olive or coconut oil, butter, *or* a combination of these oils

1 small yellow onion (finely chopped)

1 datil chile pepper (finely minced)

¼ tsp. allspice (ground)

Salt and pepper to taste

Rocotillo

On the island of Puerto Rico and in the West Indies, the most common pod type is the rocotillo. This pod is similar in shape to that of the Scotch bonnet but has a very long pedicel. It is less hot than the standard Scotch bonnet. It is perfect for seasoning "jerk" meats and authentically seasoning Puerto Rican dishes. While young, these fruits appear yellow or green in color, but they ripen into many different hues, particularly orange, brown, and red. In terms of taste, it's again a very mild heat with a moderate amount of sweetness, very much like a toned-down Scotch bonnet or habanero.

There are two different hot pepper varieties that share the same name. There's a *Capsicum baccatum* variety that originates from Peru and the *Capsicum chinense* variety. Yet, the two different varieties look nearly identical and are very similar in overall heat. To add to the confusion, there are also local variations on the names of "rocotillo" peppers in different areas of the world (not uncommon with chile peppers). Normally, a mild *C. chinense* grown on various Caribbean islands, including Cuba and the Cayman Islands, is called the rocotillo. The term has been used to describe different pod types, for example a habanero or a Scotch Bonnet pepper may be called "rocotillo" by the grower at a farmer's market . . . Now there's a real recipe for confusion! The rocotillo's appearance can be described as "slightly squished with a bulging center."

Rocotillo Mango Salsa

This salsa goes particularly well with grilled fish, chicken, or pork. The key to this simple side dish is finding fresh rocotillo peppers. In appearance, the rocotillo resembles a slightly smaller version of the incendiary habanero, the world's hottest pepper. The rocotillo has much the same fruity, mustardy flavor as the habanero, but almost none of the heat, making it an excellent chile pepper for milder salsas and chutneys.

INSTRUCTIONS

Combine the pods, mango, onion, and bell peppers in a blender or food processer and mix. Add the lime and orange juice and mix well again. Chill for at least 1 hour before serving. Serves 6 to 8.

INGREDIENTS

8 to 12 rocotillo pods (deveined, deseeded, destemmed, and chopped)

1 medium mango

1 medium red onion

1 medium red bell pepper

1 medium green bell pepper

4 tbsps. lime juice

½ cup orange juice

Jerk Sauce

Although Jamaican chefs and family cooks keep their recipes close to their chests, all of them can agree on one thing: jerk sauce should be challengingly spicy, so it's important to not skimp on the peppers in this recipe.

INSTRUCTIONS

Put all the ingredients into a food processor or a blender and process until smooth. Adjust the number of peppers and garlic cloves according to your tolerance for heat. Store the sauce in an airtight container in the refrigerator indefinitely. Use with the jerk burger recipe under the section on the Scotch bonnet or with any variety of meats. Serves 1 to 2 meals.

INGREDIENTS:

3 tbsps. jerk seasoning or 1 small Scotch bonnet pepper (deveined, deseeded, and minced)

3 tbsps. orange juice

2 tbsps. lime juice

2 tbsps. apple cider vinegar

1 tbsp. soy sauce

1 lb. ground beef

Bhut Jolokia
(Ghost Pepper)

Holy Jolokia! That's the name of the Chile Pepper Institute's famous hot sauce product line using the Bhut Jolokia, or "ghost pepper." This partnership marked the first time the Chile Pepper Institute partnered with a private company (CaJohns Fiery Foods), resulting in a partnership that is sure to cement New Mexico as the chile capital of the world. Following years of rigorous testing with High-Performance Liquid Chromatography (HPLC) by researchers at the Chile Pepper Institute, it was revealed that the heat level of the Bhut Jolokia pepper was more than 1 million SHUs—the first time a

Bhut Jolokia fruits.

chile pepper registered 1 million Scoville Heat Units in history. The Bhut Jolokia made world headlines when it was awarded the world's record as the "hottest of all spices" by Guinness World Records in September 2006. The area where it is widely grown—in the state of Assam, in northeastern India—experienced new agricultural jobs and expansion due to the increased demand for the now-famous chile pepper.

Bhut Jolokia translates from the Assam language as "ghost pepper"; it is said to be so hot that one will give up the ghost eating it. It also became the first chile pepper to be considered a "superhot" chile pepper. This plant will grow in most areas of the United States but especially enjoys a hot and humid climate. Bhut Jolokia seeds germinate best when the soil temperature is between 84° to 90°F. Plants grow to be 4 feet tall and produce a profusion of flowers. But because its pedigree, primarily being *C. chinense*, has a bit of *C. frutescens*, flower drop is common so the number of pods per plant is limited. The good news is that a few pods go a long way!

INGREDIENTS

2 tbsps. olive oil

1½ lbs. smoked sausage (e.g., Andouille or kielbasa) (cut into ½ inch slices)

2 cups yellow onions (chopped)

1 cup celery (finely chopped)

1 cup green bell peppers (deveined, deseeded, and finely chopped)

5 garlic cloves (minced)

1 jalapeno pepper (deveined, deseeded, and finely chopped)

¼ cup tomato paste

1 bay leaf

1 tsp. salt

Freshly ground black pepper

⅛ tsp. Bhut Jolokia powder

2 tbsps. garlic powder

1 tbsp. black pepper

1 tbsp. onion powder

1 tbsp. dried oregano

1 tbsp. dried thyme

5 cups chicken broth

1½ cups fresh tomatoes (peeled, deseeded, and chopped)

3 cups long-grain rice (uncooked)

1 bunch scallions (finely chopped)

½ cup fresh parsley (chopped)

Bhut Jolokia Sausage Jambalaya

Jambalaya is the perfect one-dish meal. Pair it with cornbread and wine. Be very cautious with the amount of Bhut Jolokia powder you use until you have determined your family's tolerance for heat without overwhelming the hearty pepper's flavor.

INSTRUCTIONS

In a large Dutch oven, heat the oil over medium-high heat. Add the sausage and cook, stirring frequently until browned (about 4 to 5 minutes). Using a large spoon or ladle, remove any excess oil and discard. Add the onions, celery, bell pepper, garlic, and jalapeno pepper and continue to cook, stirring occasionally until the vegetables are tender (about 4 to 6 minutes). Add the tomato paste, bay leaf, salt, pepper, the Bhut Jolokia powder, herbs, chicken stock, and tomatoes. Bring to a simmer. Then cover and reduce heat to low and cook for 40 minutes. Stir in the rice and scallions and return to a boil. Cover again and reduce heat to a low simmer. Cook undisturbed for about 20 minutes until the rice has absorbed the liquid and is tender. Remove from heat and let sit covered for 5 minutes. Remove the bay leaf and gently stir in the parsley. Let stand for another 10 to 15 minutes, covered, before serving. Serves 6.

Ghost Pepper Brownies

INGREDIENTS

1½ sticks unsalted butter (cut into tbsp.–sized pieces)

1¼ cups semisweet chocolate chips

½ cup cocoa powder

¾ cup sugar

¾ cup brown sugar (packed down)

3 large eggs (2 eggs and 1 egg yolk)

1 tsp. vanilla extract

½ tsp. salt

1 cup all–purpose flour

¼ tsp. Bhut Jolokia powder

This recipe will undoubtedly be the easiest recipe we've provided in this book because you can make it simply by purchasing your favorite packaged brownie mix and adding some Bhut Jolokia powder (a small amount!) or by purchasing a package of Dr. B's Bhut Kickin' Brownie Mix (which contains the Bhut Jolokia powder) online at the Chile Pepper Institute (https://cpi.nmsu.edu/). But just in case you want to make it from scratch, we've provided our favorite recipe.

INSTRUCTIONS

Remove the butter from the refrigerator at least one hour prior to preparing this recipe. Preheat oven to 350°F and line a 9- x 9-inch metal baking pan with parchment paper or grease and flour the pan. Combine the butter and ½ cup of the semisweet chocolate chips in a large, microwave-safe bowl. Microwave for 30 seconds. Stir well, then microwave for another 15 seconds and stir again. Repeat until the chocolate and butter are completely melted and well combined. Add the cocoa powder and both sugars, stirring until completely combined. Add the eggs, one at a time. After each addition, stir well, and then stir another 30 seconds (the more you stir your batter, the cracklier your brownie tops will be). Stir in the vanilla extract. Sprinkle salt over the batter and stir. Add the flour and stir until completely combined. Add the Bhut Jolokia powder. You cannot overmix this batter. Stir in the rest of the chocolate chips. Spread into the prepared baking pan. Optionally, for even more crackly brownies, place the baking pan with the batter in the refrigerator for 15 to 30 minutes to chill. You can skip this step if you don't have the patience to wait. Remove from the refrigerator and bake on 350°F for 30 to 35 minutes. Insert a knife or toothpick in the center of the pan. The brownies should be just slightly fudgy, but not wet with batter. Allow to cool before cutting. Serves 24.

Trinidad Moruga Scorpion

After the discovery of the Bhut Jolokia, Paul Bosland's colleagues in Trinidad and Tobago sent word that they had a chile pepper that was even hotter, the Scorpion. The Chile Pepper Institute grew out the accessions sent from Trinidad and identified the Trinidad Moruga Scorpion accession as the hottest chile pepper in the world, with an average heat of more than 1.2 million SHUs and individual plants with a heat of more than 2 million SHUs. This can be translated to the fruit having four hundred times the heat of a jalapeno. Currently, the Chile Pepper Institute recognizes the Trinidad Moruga Scorpion as the world's hottest.

Since the discovery of these two super-hot varieties, other chile peppers have claimed the throne of world's hottest chile pepper. However, for the Chile Pepper Institute to declare a chile pepper to the be world's hottest, a scientific study must be accomplished. A replicated trial with controls is grown and appropriate statistics are used to confirm the heat level to be scientifically sound. So far, no other chile pepper has been found to be hotter than the Trinidad Moruga Scorpion.

The Chile Pepper Institute has discovered what makes the super-hot chile peppers so hot. The fruits have a different structure than

Trinadad Moruga Scorpion Pepper Fruits.

those produced by "ordinary" chile peppers. Super-hot chile pepper fruits have vesicles on the fruit walls, something not found in other chile pepper varieties. These extra vesicles create additional capsa-icinoids, producing an extremely hot chile pepper. This structural difference was the result of a genetic mutation sometime in the chile peppers' past.

Prepare and cook dishes with this pepper with extreme caution. Once the peppers start heating up, the resulting aromas can sting the eyes and lungs. Consider using a mask and gloves WHENEVER working with peppers.

Tomato Basil Soup

This soup makes a great first course for dinner or an accompaniment to your favorite sandwich.

INSTRUCTIONS

Warm the oil in a pot over medium heat. Add the onions, peppers, ginger, and garlic. Sauté until the onions are tender, about 5 minutes Add the tomatoes, fish sauce, and curry. Bring to a boil, then reduce the heat to a simmer. Add the coconut milk and basil and cook for 10 to 15 minutes Puree in a food processor or with an immersion blender. Ladle the soup into bowls, garnish with basil, and serve. Serves 4.

INGREDIENTS

1 tbsp. olive oil

1 onion (diced)

Trinidad Moruga Scorpion pods (deveined, deseeded, and diced)

1 tbsp. ginger (grated)

3 garlic cloves (minced)

One 28-oz. can whole, peeled tomatoes (undrained)

1 tbsp. fish sauce

1½ tbsps. curry powder

One 13.5-oz. can coconut milk

¼ cup basil (julienned) plus more for garnish

Aloochoka (Caribbean Mashed Potatoes)

INGREDIENTS

1 lb. potatoes (washed and peeled)

Salt to taste

1 tsp. oil

1 onion (finely diced)

3 garlic cloves (minced)

1 fresh Scotch bonnet chile pepper

Try this Caribbean twist on mashed potatoes. If the dish is too hot for your taste, try a milder chile pepper for flavor but not heat.

INSTRUCTIONS

In a large pot of water, cook the potatoes, until soft. Drain and mash them, then return to the pot and add salt. In a small skillet, heat the oil. Add the onion and garlic and sauté until soft. Add the chile pepper to the onion and garlic and sauté again, briefly. Quickly combine with the mashed potatoes and serve immediately. Serves 4.

Appendix

Chile Infusions

The Teaching Garden chile peppers contain heat levels from mild to super-hot. Plus, each variety also has unique flavor profiles that you can use to flavor your dishes in special ways. One way to experience their heat levels and flavor profiles to find those chile peppers that you especially like is by making chile pepper infusions with your favorite liquids (tea, coffee, vinegar, honey, water, soda, alcohol, etc.) With an infusion, you can experiment and learn which chile peppers to grow in your future garden plots and have a better idea of the form (fresh, frozen, roasted, dried, etc.) and quantity of peppers to use in a specific recipe. Infusions all stem from the same process—transferring chile pepper varieties right out of your garden or favorite farmers' market into a liquid. Below are three variations on this theme. You can experiment in many different directions by varying the variety and amount of chile pepper, the type and volume of liquid, and the amount of time you let the infusion sit. Keep good notes: you can use that information in the future in both the kitchen and the garden.

Chile-Infused Vinegar

INSTRUCTIONS

Wash the fresh chile peppers and place them in a clean jar to within 1 inch of the top. Fill the jar with vinegar until the pods are submerged. Seal lid tightly. Allow ingredients to blend for a week in a cool, dark place.

USES

Pour a little of the chile pepper infused vinegar into a small pitcher and combine with an equal part olive oil to use as a salad dressing. Or you can pour chile pepper-infused vinegar on pulled pork or other meat as a marinade.

INGREDIENTS

One 8-oz. clean canning jar with lid

Handful of one or more varieties of fresh or dried chile peppers of your choice

6 oz. of your favorite vinegar

Chile-Infused Honey

INGREDIENTS

One 8-oz. clean canning jar with lid

Handful of one or more varieties of fresh or dried chile peppers of your choice

6 oz. honey

INSTRUCTIONS

Fill the jar with the chile peppers to within 1 inch of top. Pour the honey in a saucepan, watching it closely, and warm over medium heat or pour into a microwaveable glass and heat in the microwave until the honey is liquefied. Pour over pods into the jar. Seal lid tightly and allow to cool. Store at room temperature.

USES

Pour chile pepper-infused honey over yogurt, ice cream, waffles, biscuits, or fresh fruit.

Chile-Infused Oils

INSTRUCTIONS

Combine the chile pepper with oil in a saucepan and heat over a medium-high heat until the pods begin to sizzle or about 1 to 2 minutes. Add optional seasonings at this point. Allow the mixture to cool completely. Then pour into the glass jar, sealing the lid tightly. Place in a cool, dark place for 3 to 4 days. If desired, strain the seeds and pieces from the oil before using.

USES

Use infusion to marinate meat or tofu or as a dipping sauce or condiment. It can be used in most recipes in place of plain oil where a spicy flavor is preferred.

INGREDIENTS

One 8-oz. clean canning jar with lid

Handful dried and chopped chile peppers

6 oz. neutral flavored oil such as canola

Small amounts of seasonings (e.g., garlic slices or peppercorns, optional)

Making Chile Powder

INSTRUCTIONS

Cut washed green or red peppers lengthwise in half so the flesh is open. Opening the pods will help them to dry out more quickly and evenly. Place a layer of parchment paper on a cookie sheet and lay the peppers out in a single layer across the sheet. Dry peppers at 200°F. Keep an eye on them and remove those that are dry, so they don't burn. It can take 1 to 3 hours to dry all the peppers depending on the extent to which they were dry when you picked them. Allow to cool until you can touch them. Crush the pods in a plastic bag using a rolling pin. Sift until larger pieces are removed and a fine powder remains. Store in an airtight container and use to flavor meats, casseroles, and appetizers.

How to Roast Chile on the Grill or in the Oven

To roast and peel chile peppers on a grill, lay pods on their sides on a barbeque grill. Turn the flame on high and char the pods, turning them with tongs, until the skins are blackened, 3 to 6 minutes.

To broil the pods, preheat the broiler. Broil pods about 2 inches from heat on the rack of a broiler pan. Turn them frequently until the skins are blistered and charred, 8 to 12 minutes.

Transfer the pods, roasted by either method, to a bowl and let stand, covered with a lid, until cool enough to handle. Wearing rubber gloves, peel the pods and cut off their tops. Discard the seeds and ribs. Set aside.

How to Freeze Chile

Wash the pods and allow to dry before preparing them for freezing by laying them on a towel or lightly patting them dry. If working with small pods, you may choose to freeze them whole using freezer bags or containers. Larger pods are easier to use later if the pods are sliced opened and the seeds and membrane are removed. Pods can also be roasted on the grill or in the oven prior to freezing. If prepared after roasting, they are usually deskinned and sliced open, with the membrane and seeds removed. When freezing larger lengths of pods, consider laying the strips in a freezer bag or container only 1 or 2 layers thick for easier removal, once frozen. Another option is the chop the pods into bite-sized pieces and spread the pieces flat in the bag or container so sections can be easily broken off if you want to use only a small portion. Label your containers with a date and the name of the chile pepper so you don't lose track of your supply! Depending on your freezer setting, you can generally use your frozen peppers for up to a year.

Index

271

Turkish seasoning
    —Turkish Kabobs with Aleppo
        Pepper, *126*, 127

Urfa biber pepper, 123–124

Vasquez de Coronado, Francisco, 47
vinegar. *See also* balsamic vinegar
    —Chile-Infused, 264
    —Chile Pepper Vinegar Sauce, *175*,
        175–176
    —Kinilaw na tuna (Raw Tuna Sal-
        ad), *181*, 181–182
    —rice, *137*, 137–138
vitamin C, 37

watercress
    —Avocado and Scrambled Egg
        Brunch Bowl, *184*, 185

wax pepper. *See* Hungarian wax
weed control, 1, 2, *2*
wheat bran
    —Chocolate Chip Cookies, *107*,
        107–108
whipped topping, 158
wild peppers, about, 1–2, *3*, 4, 16

Yellow Mole Chicken, 87
yogurt
    —Dukkah Flatbread, 218–219
    —Yogurt Dip, *126*, 127
yuzu juice, 200

Library of Congress Control Number: 2022947820

Founded in 1889, the University of New Mexico sits on the traditional homelands of the Pueblo of Sandia. The original peoples of New Mexico—Pueblo, Navajo, and Apache—since time immemorial have deep connections to the land and have made significant contributions to the broader community statewide. We honor the land itself and those who remain stewards of this land throughout the generations and acknowledge our committed relationship to Indigenous peoples. We gratefully recognize our history.

Cover photographs: courtesy of Acton Crawford, licensed under CC by 2.0.
Designed by Felicia Cedillos
Composed in Utopia 11.75/17